The
Thanksgiving
Book

The Thanksgiving Book

by LUCILLE RECHT PENNER

*Illustrated with prints and photographs
selected by Lucille Recht Penner
and arranged by Al Lichtenberg*

C. 1

HASTINGS HOUSE, *Publishers* NEW YORK

Library of Congress Cataloging in Publication Data
Penner, Lucille Recht.
    The Thanksgiving book.

    Bibliography: p.
    Includes index.
    1. Thanksgiving Day.   I. Title.
GT4975.P46   1984   394.2'683   84-518
ISBN 0-8038-7228-3
ISBN 0-8038-9291-8 lib. ed.

Hastings House, Publishers
260 Fifth Avenue
New York, New York 10001

Distributed to the trade by:
Kampmann & Company, Inc.
New York, New York

Printed in the United States of America
10 9 8 7 6 5 4 3 2 1

Contents

Acknowledgments

For their help with my research, I thank the historical societies of Vermont, Maryland, Maine, and Hawaii; the Biblioteca General de Puerto Rico; the St. Thomas-St. John Chamber of Commerce; the Pennsylvania German Society; the Public Information Department of Old Sturbridge Village; the Agricultural History Branch of the United States Department of Agriculture; the Schwenkfelder Library; the National Turkey Federation; the Pennsylvania Folklife Society; Plimoth Plantation; the Pilgrim Society; the Bureau of Indian Affairs of the United States Department of the Interior; the Department of Anthropology of the Smithsonian Institute; the Consulate General of India; and the Swedish Information Service. I am grateful to Jay Anderson for permission to use material from his article, "Partakers of Plenty: A Study of the First Thanksgiving." For permission to include recipes from *Fanny Pierson Crane, Her Receipts, 1796: Confections, Savouries, and Drams* (1974), I thank the Montclair Historical Society, Box 322, Montclair, N.J. 07042. The recipes for Molasses Pie, Neversink, Turkey Scallop, Green Corn Soup, and Popcorn Cake Mennonite, from *The Pennsylvania Dutch Cookbook* by J. George Frederick (1935 and 1971), are included by permission of Dover Publications, Inc. The Plymouth Antiquarian Society permitted me to include the recipe for Bradford Plum Pudding from *The Plymouth Colony Cookbook* (1973). I am grateful for the help of Elise Berkower and Shereen Greenberg, and especially for that of my editor, Judy Donnelly.

to Benjamin and Daniel

A portrait of a wild turkey by John James Audubon (1785–1851).

CHAPTER ONE

Of Turkeys and Touchdowns

WHO invented Thanksgiving?
Was it the Pilgrims, those few dozen astonishing people, who fought hardship and disease—who survived fear and loneliness—to plant the seeds of America?

Partly, yes. At their first Thanksgiving, in 1621, the Pilgrims thanked God for their survival in America. They were joined by 90 Indians, ceremonially smeared with bear grease, who provided the deer meat for this famous feast.

But thanksgiving ceremonies are far older than that. Did they begin in England, where the Pilgrims came from? A thousand and more years ago, English farmers were giving thanks for successful harvests. They believed that a spirit— the corn-spirit—lived in the crops and made them grow. And they had magic rituals to keep the corn-spirit from getting angry when harvest time came.

But even that is not the beginning of the thanksgiving story. Thanksgiving goes back to the ancient Greeks and Romans, back to the ancient Hebrews. Back to ancient Egyptian farmers, who wept as they harvested their crops so that the spirits would not be angry at them. Back to ancient China, where thanksgiving was celebrated as the birthday of the moon.

In fact, thanksgiving ceremonies come from every age, and practically everywhere on earth. Everywhere, thanksgiving celebrates a seeming miracle—the harvest.

And everywhere, thanksgiving was—in addition to a religious occasion—an important social occasion, too. With the long, lonely months of farm work done and the crops safely in, people at last had time for feasts, games, songs, and dances. The natives of Hawaii enjoyed their thanksgiving for four months! During this time the people were not supposed to do any work at all.

For us, turkey has become a symbol of Thanksgiving. But the thanksgiving turkey has been around much longer

The ancient Mayans celebrated with turkey hundreds of years ago. This drawing is from a 16th century Mexican manuscript.

"The Cornell Farm" by Edward Hicks (1780–1849). Thanksgiving gave Americans an opportunity to celebrate the abundance of the new land.

than most people imagine. The ancient Mayan people celebrated their harvest with a turkey-and-squash feast. When there wasn't enough turkey to go around, they added the other kind of meat they raised—dog. Turkey was considered the choicer meat, and was always placed on top.

Today, Thanksgiving means games, especially football games. And games were part of the Pilgrims' first Thanksgiving, too—including an archery display by the Indians. Games have been a part of the holiday in almost every time and place.

Thanksgiving today also means parades—everything from grade school marching bands to the giant Macy's parade in New York City. Thousands of New Yorkers get

Grandma Moses, who first began painting in her 70's, became well-known for her pictures of country life and family holidays, such as "Thanksgiving Turkey."

up before dawn to claim choice spots along the Macy's route, and millions of other Americans watch the parade on television. There are bands, elaborately decorated floats, and gigantic helium-filled balloons—some the size of tall buildings.

Thanksgiving parades have always been festive in spirit. Farmers in ancient Egypt, in ancient Rome, in medieval England, paraded home their flower-decorated harvest from the fields to the village. When they arrived, there was singing, dancing, and feasting.

This book tells the story of wonderful and unusual thanksgivings among ancient people, through the Middle Ages, and up to the present. It tells about the delicious foods of the holiday, their interesting origins, and how to cook them.

It shows how—in many of the things we do, as in many of the foods we eat—our Thanksgiving celebration joins us with all of humanity who came before us, who planted and harvested, who made merry in their time.

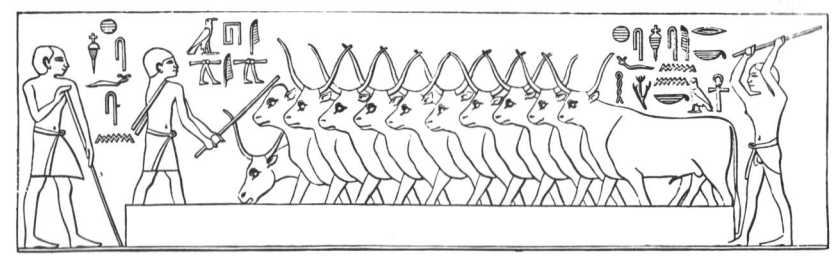

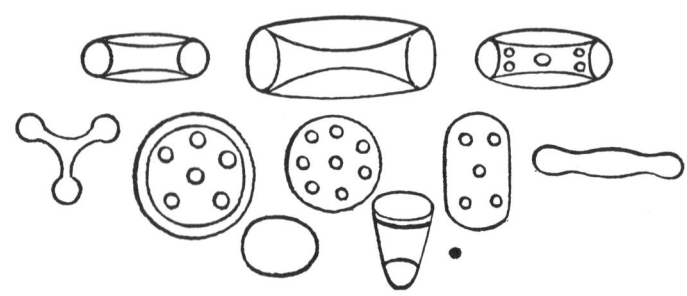

Ancient Egyptians at harvest time. Above: Working in the fields. Center: Egyptian breads took many shapes. Below: Making bread from harvested grain.

CHAPTER TWO

Ancient Harvest Celebrations

Come, ye thankful people, come,
Raise the Song of Harvest Home.

—HENRY ALFORD,
Thanksgiving Day

As LONG as people have been raising crops—since before earliest recorded history—they have been celebrating the harvest.

It is easy to understand why. When a community had only the food that it could produce itself, the success or failure of the harvest was a matter of life or death. Its annual recurrence seemed a miraculous blessing.

Harvest ceremonies sprang up all over the world. Though ancient farmers lived in widely scattered places, they shared many beliefs about the harvest.

They believed that the rhythms of the growing year were related to those of human life. People saw birth and death all around them, an endless cycle. And their crops seemed to follow the same pattern.

Crops were "born" from under the ground and "died" in the harvest. The fact that they grew from underground, which many ancient people regarded as the home of the dead, suggested that the crops must contain spirits. People believed that at the time of the harvest these spirits must be either pacified or destroyed, or they would take revenge against the farmers who harvested them.

Long before there were formal religions, people prayed to the spirits of their crops, and to the spirits of the rain and sun on which their crops depended. And even after the major religions of today were established, many people who believed in them also continued to practice the old religious rituals of the harvest.

The Chinese

According to the Chinese lunar (moon) calendar, the harvest moon becomes a full moon on the fifteenth day of the eighth month. The Chinese believed that the moon is brighter and more perfectly round on this date than on any other day of the year. They regarded it as the moon's birthday.

The moon's birthday was the start of their harvest festival, Chung Ch'ui. They connected the moon with the harvest because they thought of her as a farmer. At night, while the sun (her husband) was gone, she plowed the sky from horizon to horizon.

Her birthday was a family affair. In each home, five plates were arranged on an altar. In the center of each plate was a "moon cake," surrounded by round fruits.

The women made these moon cakes from the new grain of the harvest. The cakes were as round and yellow as the moon, with red or green decorations. Yellow was a sacred color, green was the color of immortality, and red was the

Chinese farmers working in a rice field.

color of happiness. Each cake was stamped with the picture of a rabbit, because it was a rabbit, not a man, that the Chinese thought they saw on the full moon's face.

Outdoors, while musicians played in the moonlight, families feasted on roast pork, fruit, and the delicious moon cakes. Games were organized for the children. The celebration lasted three days. The Chinese believed that during this time flowers fell from the moon, and that people who were sharp-eyed enough to see them would have good fortune. The women would have many children, and the men would become rich.

Chung Ch'ui, like the American Thanksgiving, was not only a harvest festival but also a time for expressing thanks. People thanked the gods for the harvest. They also thanked the spirits of their ancestors, who they believed watched over and influenced their lives.

But Chung Ch'ui was also the occasion to give thanks for something else—an event that was said to have happened on the same day of the year in a time remotely ancient.

According to this legend, China was once conquered by enemy armies. The invading soldiers moved into people's homes and ate their food. The Chinese suffered and starved. At last they decided that they must kill the invaders and free their country.

In order to succeed, they knew they had to rise up all at once. But how could they be sure of doing that? Finally a clever way was found. The women baked moon cakes and distributed them to every family. Inside each cake was a note, telling the time to attack.

When the given moment arrived, every Chinese household attacked the enemy soldiers who had taken over its home. Taken by surprise, the enemy was easily defeated.

And that, says the legend, was why the Chinese ate "moon cakes" every year on the anniversary of their victory.

The Greeks and the Romans

The Greeks believed in many gods and goddesses, each of whom ruled a certain part of nature or a particular human activity.

A Roman breadbasket.

The goddess responsible for making crops grow was Demeter, the corn goddess. ("Corn" is used here in the British sense of the word, to mean all kinds of grain, including wheat, oats, and barley.)

The myth of Demeter is a beautiful explanation of the cycle of the growing year. One day Demeter's daughter, Persephone, was gathering flowers in a meadow. She was reaching to pick a beautiful narcissus when suddenly the ground opened up beneath her. Hades, the god of the underworld, appeared. He seized Persephone and carried the screaming girl down into the earth to be his bride.

High atop Mount Olympus, the home of the gods and goddesses, Demeter heard her daughter's scream. Frantic, she rushed down to help her. But Persephone was nowhere to be found. Demeter searched for nine days and nights without stopping to eat or sleep. Finally Helios, the sun, who had seen the whole thing, took pity on her and told her what had happened to her daughter.

Demeter was so overcome with grief that she stopped making the crops grow. Soon people all over the world were in danger of starving.

Not only were they unable to feed themselves, they were also unable to make harvest offerings to the gods. And

this finally angered Zeus, the king of the gods. He commanded Hades to return Persephone to her mother.

Unfortunately, while Persephone was in the underworld she had eaten six forbidden pomegranate seeds. Hades insisted that she had to remain with him six months out of every year—one month for each seed she had eaten. For the other six months she could return to her mother.

And that was what happened. Demeter was overjoyed for the six months of every year that her daughter was with her. Gladly she made the crops grow.

But for the six months that her daughter had to go down to the underworld, Demeter was again stricken with grief and would bring no harvests. And that explains why, in winter, seeds must lie trapped in the cold earth for six months—like Persephone herself—waiting for the time when they can rise into the sunshine.

The Greek festival honoring Demeter was called the *Thesmosphoria*. It was held in the autumn, when seeds for next year's crop were about to be planted. All the participants in this festival were married women, probably because the Greeks sensed a connection between child-bearing and the raising of crops.

On the first day of the festival, the women built leafy

shelters, furnished with couches made from plants. On the second day they fasted to show that they shared Demeter's sorrow at her daughter's being taken down into the underworld.

On the third day the women held a feast to celebrate Persephone's annual return to her mother. They offered the goddess special gifts of seed corn, cakes, fruit, honeycombs, and choice pigs. They hoped that, in her gratitude for these gifts, Demeter would grant them a good harvest.

Roman civilization in general, and Roman religion in particular, were strongly influenced by the Greeks. The Roman corn goddess was very much like the Greek one. She was called Ceres, and the word "cereal" comes from her name.

The Romans worshiped Ceres at a harvest festival called the *Cerelia*, held each year on October 4. They offered her the first fruits of the harvests and a fine sow. Then they held a joyous celebration—playing music, parading through the fields, participating in games and sports, and sharing a huge thanksgiving feast.

A Roman festival to honor the goddess Ceres, as pictured by a 17th century artist.

The Hebrews

The ancient Hebrew festival of *Succot*, first celebrated more than 3,000 years ago, is still celebrated around the world by Jewish families today.

In the Bible, Succot has two names. One is *Hag ha Succot*, the Feast of Tabernacles. This name springs from the Biblical account of how, after releasing them from slavery in Egypt, God made the Hebrews wander for forty years before letting them enter the Promised Land. During this time of homelessness they lived in tiny huts of branches, easy to assemble and take apart and carry on to the next stopping place. The huts were called *succot*, or "tabernacles"—hence the Feast of Tabernacles.

Succot begins in the autumn, on the fifteenth day of the Hebrew month of Tishri, five days after the holiday of Yom Kippur. It lasts for eight days. On the first two

An 18th century family celebrating Succot, *the Hebrew harvest festival.*

days, people build small huts of branches, meant to recall the tabernacles of their ancestors. In order to show that these are temporary, movable structures, the branches are not driven into the ground, and the foliage on the roof is spaced to let the starlight in.

Then the inside walls of the huts are hung with apples, grapes, corn, pomegranates, and other fruits and vegetables. For Succot is also a harvest festival, and the other name given to it in the Bible is *Hag ha Asif*—the Feast of Ingathering.

In religious services held during Succot, Jews thank God for creating plants. Four particular plants, each of which has special symbolic meaning, are used in the ceremony:

> —The *estrog*, a fragrant and delicious citrus fruit, resembles a large lemon. It symbolizes people who are well educated and also do good deeds.

> —The *lulav* is a branch of the date palm tree. Its fruit is good to eat, but it has no scent. It symbolizes people who are educated but do not do good deeds.

> —The *hadas* is a myrtle branch. It smells good but has no edible fruit. It stands for those who do good deeds but are not educated.

> —The *aravah* is a willow branch, having neither fruit nor scent. It symbolizes people who neither have education nor do good deeds.

As you see, a pleasant taste is associated with a good education, and a pleasing smell is associated with good deeds. To acquire knowledge and to perform good deeds are, in Jewish tradition, the two marks of a virtuous person.

The branches of the date palm, willow, and myrtle are bound together and held in the right hand, while the *estrog* is held in the left hand. Waving the branches toward all points of the compass is said to bring good luck. They are passed around so that everyone has a chance to hold them. Then a special blessing is said.

In the joyous celebration of Succot, as in the other festivals we have examined, we see the theme of harvest festivity mingled with the theme of thanksgiving for blessings.

The Egyptians

One of the most important gods worshiped by the ancient Eygptians was Min, the god of vegetation and fertility. A special harvest festival was celebrated in his honor every spring, which was the Egyptians' harvest season.

The festival of Min featured a great public parade. The Pharaoh himself took part, followed by a white bull—Min's sacred animal. Behind the bull came an enormous statue of Min, carried by priests. After the statue came another

Ancient Egyptians gathering okra and fig

priest with a bundle of choice lettuces, which were regarded as the god's favorite plant.

When the parade was over, a great feast was held. There were music, dancing, and sports—including a greased pole-climbing contest. It was a day for joy.

But at the time they actually harvested their corn, the Egyptian farmers wept and pretended to be grief-stricken. This was to deceive a spirit that they believed lived in the corn. They feared that the spirit would be angry with them for cutting the corn in which it lived, and letting cattle trample the corn on the threshing room floor.

So they acted as though cutting the corn caused them sorrow rather than joy, beating their fists against their chests and crying out a mournful chant. The Greeks who heard this traditional chant gave it the name *maneros*.

Throughout the ancient world, widely separated groups of farmers created similar rituals to deal with the powerful spirits which, they believed, caused the crops to grow or shriveled them in the fields. They performed these rituals with both fear and joy. A successful harvest meant life itself.

with the help of trained monkeys.

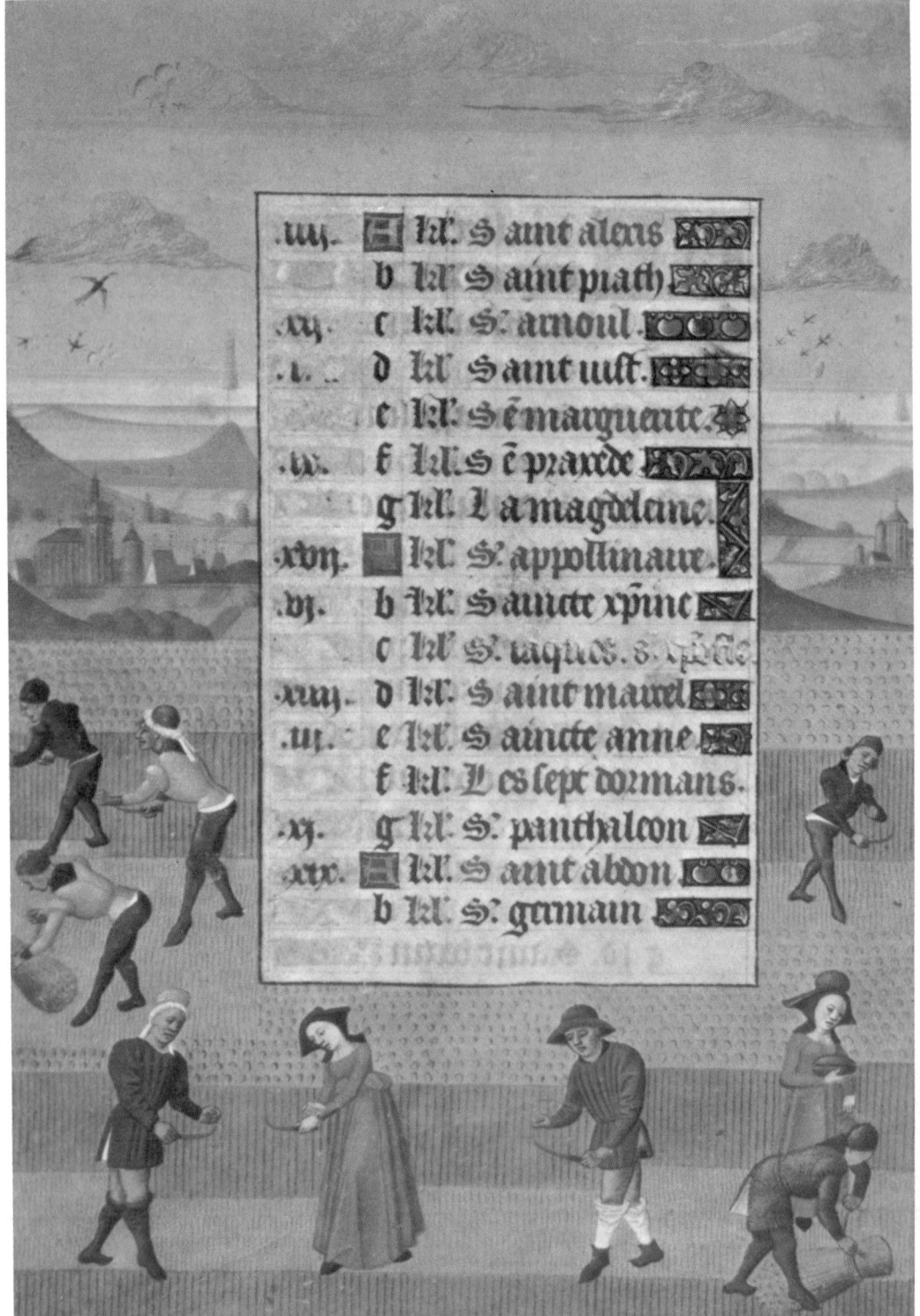

A harvest scene from a medieval manuscript.

CHAPTER THREE

The Spirit of the Corn

THE ANCIENT fear of the corn-spirit lasted throughout the Middle Ages. Even as late as the nineteenth century, some farmers practiced charms and rituals to pacify the spirit, and thereby ensure a good harvest for the coming year.

For instance, the people of Estonia, in eastern Europe, would not eat bread made from newly harvested corn until they had first pretended to take a bite from a piece of iron. This was to make them so strong that the corn-spirit would be unable to hurt them.

When corn tassels blew in the wind, German farmers told each other, "The Corn Mother is running through the fields." Children who wanted to play in the fields were warned, "Don't go there. The Corn Mother will get you." After they had harvested their corn and ground it into flour, German farmers threw handfuls of it from the rooftops into the strong autumn wind, chanting, "There you are, wind! Cook meal for your child!"

Seventeenth century farmers with the fruits of their harvest.

An engraving by J. Matham.

Bringing home the harvest; a drawing from an old songbook.

Many rituals involved the cutting of the last sheaf of corn. It was widely believed that, as the corn was cut, the corn-spirit fled before the advancing sickles, running from plant to plant. Finally it was cornered in the last plant in the field, and captured in the last sheaf to be cut.

Farmers often tried to get rid of the corn-spirit by gathering their harvest before their neighbors did. When they had trapped the spirit in the last sheaf, the fastest runner among the harvesters quickly grabbed it up. He ran with it to the fields of a neighbor who hadn't yet finished harvesting, and tossed it into the standing grain. This neighbor, in turn, tried to gather his harvest quickly enough so that he could deliver the angry spirit to someone else's field.

In Sweden, the grain from the last sheaf was sometimes baked into a cake shaped like a little girl. Everyone in the farmer's household got a piece of it. As they ate, they believed they were eating the corn-spirit, which they thought of as a young girl.

Polish farmers made the last sheaf of corn into an elab-

orate crown called a "Wienjec." It was splendidly decorated with flowers, nuts, apples, and sometimes even a gingerbread cake. A girl, wearing the crown, led a procession of harvesters to the farmhouse door. There the farmer threw buckets of water at her until she was thoroughly drenched. The water was a charm, meant to ensure rain for the coming year's crops.

A farmer of the Middle Ages with his scythe.

In some parts of England, it was believed that cutting the last plant killed the corn-spirit, and nobody wanted to take full responsibility for such a terrible act. So the harvesters stood in a circle around the last plant, and all together threw their sickles at it until it was "slain."

In other parts of England, farmers observed an old custom called "Crying the Neck." Originally, this was probably a kind of mourning for the last sheaf. When the last of the corn was cut, one of the field workers braided it into a bundle called "the Neck." With both hands he held it over his head, then slowly lowered it to the ground

The other workers, standing in a circle around him, removed their hats. They bent to the ground, touching the stubble of the harvested corn. Then, as they slowly stood up and lifted their hats in the air, they called out in a musical chant, "The Neck, the Neck!" At the same time, "the Neck" was lifted high into the air. The entire ritual was repeated three times.

Afterward there was laughing and cheering. Then someone snatched "the Neck" and ran as fast as he could to the farmhouse door. A girl waited there with a pail of water. If he managed to get by her he was allowed to kiss

her. If not, she soaked him with the water—again, a rain charm.

Sometimes farmers "caught" the corn-spirit by making the last sheaf into a doll. This doll was believed to have magical powers. Depending on how people imagined the corn-spirit—in different places she was thought of as a grandmother, a pregnant woman, a maiden, and a baby— the doll might be called the Mother, the Hag, the Granny, the Kern Puppet, Mell Doll, or Harvest Queen.

Sometimes farmers decorated the doll with ribbons, yarn, and flowers, or even dressed it in clothes. It was hung on the farmhouse wall until the time came to plow the earth for next year's crops. Then the farmer's wife cut it into pieces and brought it to the fields as food for the horses. Or else she burned it, and the farmer plowed its ashes into the fields to bring luck with future harvests.

In some places the harvesters threw the carefully prepared doll into the river. They hoped that, just as the corn-

A boisterous Harvest Home in 19th century England.

spirit doll was soaked in the river, the new crops would be soaked with life-giving rain. This was a rain charm. Such charms are called imitative magic. The theory behind them is that performing a certain act will cause another act of the same kind—an imitation of the first act—to happen.

In the autumn, English farmers held a feast called Harvest Home. When the last of the corn was cut, everyone helped pile it onto a cart. They decorated it with green branches, flowers, and ribbons, and chose a Lord and Lady of the Harvest to ride in it.

As the cart was drawn home to the farmhouse, the field workers walked alongside, cheering and laughing and ringing bells. Children ate slices of plum cake. People hiding behind bushes along the path of the cart jumped out and threw buckets of water at it as it passed—one more charm to bring rain. The Lord and Lady of the Harvest were usually drenched with water by the time the cart reached the garland-decorated barn.

But everyone was merry, because a huge feast was waiting. Frumenty, a wheat pudding made with boiled milk and raisins, was usually served. If the harvest had been especially good, there might also be a roast beef and plum pudding.

After they had eaten, the harvesters danced and played games. Sometimes two men dressed up as the Old Sow, using a head stuffed with prickly branches to butt the other feasters, who laughed and tried to run away. The merry-making lasted well into the night.

Here is one of the songs they sang:

> *The boughs do shake and the bells do ring,*
> *So merrily comes our harvest in,*
> *Our harvest in, our harvest in,*
> *So merrily comes our harvest in.*
>
> *Harvest Home! Harvest Home!*
> *We've plowed, we've sowed,*
> *We've reaped, we've mowed,*
> *We've brought home every load,*
> *Hip, hip, hip, Harvest Home!*

There were some who disapproved of such riotous celebrations. These were the Puritans—strictly religious, sternly moral people. It's from them that we get the word "puritanical," signifying their preference for plain living and their belief that many pleasures are sinful.

Among the Pilgrim settlers of America, the puritanical strain was strong. Puritanism became firmly established in New England. But no matter how much the Pilgrims disapproved of the English Harvest Home, their memory of it probably influenced their creation of our American Thanksgiving.

FRUMENTY

An old English saying goes, "The frumenty pot welcomes home the harvest cart." This hearty pudding was a popular dish at Harvest Home celebrations.

1¾ cups milk	1 egg yolk
½ teaspoon almond extract	¼ cup raisins
2 tablespoons honey	ground saffron (optional)
1 cup cracked wheat	

Mix the milk, almond extract, and honey in a heavy saucepan. Bring to a boil. Add the cracked wheat and reduce the heat to low. Cover and cook, stirring occasionally, until the liquid is absorbed, about 15 minutes. Remove from the heat. Stir in the egg yolk. Add the raisins, a pinch of saffron, and mix well. Serve hot or cold.   *Serves 4.*

A portrait of the Mayan corn god, carved in stone.

CHAPTER FOUR

Indian Harvest Festivals: South America

ABOUT 20,000 years ago, humans first reached the Americas, crossing a land bridge that then connected Asia and Alaska. Eventually hundreds of tribes settled in North and Central and South America.

For many centuries, these tribes wandered in search of their food. They followed herds of animals across the plains, or roved through forests seeking edible plants. No place could be their home for long. When the local food supply was exhausted, they had to move on.

Agriculture, which permits people to stay in one place and grow (not find) their food, is necessary for the development of large, complex civilizations. It permits the building of permanent homes, and eventually cities. It creates a predictable schedule of work, so that time may be set aside for crafts and industry, experiment and commerce.

Indians planting corn (left) and picking corn (right).

Agriculture developed in stages. At first, people simply began to protect edible wild plants from animals, and from other tribes.

Then they began to clear surrounding vegetation away from their favorite plants. This gave the plants more room to grow, and let them take more water and nutrients from the soil.

Finally, people gathered the plants (or their seeds) and planted them nearer to their homes—the crucial step in the development of agricultural civilization.

South American Indians grew potatoes, sweet potatoes, pineapple, and peanuts. North American Indians grew Jerusalem artichokes and strawberries. Indian farmers were so skillful that all the important crops native to America were being cultivated by the time the first European explorers arrived.

The most important of these crops by far—the one upon which many tribes depended almost completely—was what the English called "maize," or "Indian corn."

So far in this book, we have been using the word *corn* in its old, general sense, meaning grain of any kind. In England, "corn" usually meant barley, wheat, or rye; in Scotland, it usually meant oats.

But in this chapter, "corn" means maize—"Indian corn"—our own familiar corn on the cob, and its direct ancestors.

Corn was probably first grown in South America, very

likely in Peru. By the time the Europeans came, it was being raised throughout the hemisphere.

Though it evolved from a wild grass, corn must be planted and cultivated. If farmers stopped growing it, the plant would quickly become extinct. Many tribes, seeing that corn could not grow wild like other plants, believed that it must have been specially created by the gods as a gift to mankind.

Though tasty, nutritious, and easy to grow, corn is not a perfect food. It has too little of certain nutrients, such as niacin. As a result, people whose diet depends *too* much on corn may develop a disease called pellagra. But corn has served marvelously well as the principal food of a well-rounded diet. Not only has it fed people, it has permitted the development of entire societies.

The Mayans and the Aztecs were the first to grow corn on a large scale. They ate it fresh, pounded it into flour for bread and tortillas, and dried and stored it for future use. Freed from the need to hunt or forage for their food, they had the time and energy to develop complex civilizations. They became learned in mathematics and astronomy. Though they never invented the wheel or made metal tools, they built great cities of stone in the jungles of Central America.

Aztec corn.

Seventeenth century explorers were delighted at the foods of the New World.

Everything depended on corn, and corn depended on adequate rainfall. So these early American farmers did all they could to make it rain. They wept loudly. They bled themselves. They mimicked thunder and the croaking of frogs. These were forms of imitative magic, like the rituals practiced by farmers in England.

Many of the Mayans' religious festivals reveal the importance that corn held for them. They held a festival of Yum Kax (their corn god, who, they believed, had actually created them out of kernels of corn); they held a rain festival; and they held—after the gathering of the crops—a celebration of harvest home. This last, like the English harvest home, was a time of singing and dancing. Popcorn was made from the newly harvested corn, and young girls threw handfuls of it at the spectators.

The Aztecs' civilization, like the Mayans', was built

upon corn. So it was natural that one of their chief deities was the goddess Xilonen, "She Who Always Walked and Remained as Fresh and Tender as a Young Ear of Corn."

Xilonen also had two other names. In good years she was called Chalchiuhcihuatl, which means "Woman of Precious Stone," in appreciation of the wonderful harvests she brought. In lean years, she was called Chicomecoatl, "Serpent of Seven Heads." This name referred to the cruel side of her nature. When crops were poor, the Aztecs believed that the angry goddess had ordered corn seeds to freeze in the ground instead of sprouting.

They celebrated her festival only in years when the crops were good. Its date was September 15. A slave girl represented the goddess. She was dressed in an elaborate costume, and adorned with precious stones. Her face was painted yellow and red, and she was crowned with a hat that had bright green plumes suggesting the tassels of corn.

An ancient Mexican pottery figure of a ballplayer. Games were part of the earliest harvest festivals in America.

A week before the festival, following a banquet, the Aztecs began a near-total fast. They ate only scraps of old tortillas, and drank only water. All week, the slave girl danced. Then, when the day of Xilonen arrived at last, the girl was slain as a sacrifice to the goddess. Thereupon an enormous feast was held.

AZTEC PUMPKIN FLOWER TORTILLAS

The Aztecs used pumpkin flowers to flavor puddings, soups, and tacos. Here is a simple vegetable dish to make when pumpkin plants are flowering. Squash blossoms can be used instead.

2 cups pumpkin flowers	*1 cup tomato, chopped*
2 tablespoons corn oil	*12 tortillas*
½ onion, chopped	*1 cup heavy cream*
½ cup green chiles, chopped	*1½ cups cheddar cheese, grated*
1 cup fresh corn kernels	

Preheat oven to 350°. Butter a 9 by 13 inch baking dish.

Wash the flowers gently in cold water. Pat dry. Remove and slice the petals finely. Set aside.

Heat the oil. Add the onion and cook until golden. Add the chiles, corn, and tomato. Cover and simmer 5 minutes over low heat.

Remove from the heat and stir in the chopped flower petals. Place 3 tablespoons of the flower mixture in the middle of each tortilla. Roll up tightly and place, seam side down, in the buttered baking dish. Pour cream over the top. Sprinkle with the grated cheese. Bake until the cheese browns, 15 to 20 minutes.

Serves 6 to 8.

MAYAN CHOCOLATE DRINK

The Mayans called the first chocolate drink that they made from cacao beans *kakau*, which means "bitter water." This sacred drink was given only to priests. Later, chocolate water mixed with honey became a favorite drink of the rich. When the Spanish arrived, they mixed chocolate water with sugar and milk and drank it hot. In Mexico today, craftspeople make a carved wooden beater called a *molinillo* which is used to whip air into chocolate drinks.

2 ounces unsweetened chocolate *¼ teaspoon cinnamon*
2 tablespoons honey *2 cups water or milk*
½ teaspoon vanilla

Melt the chocolate over very low heat. Stir in the honey, vanilla, cinnamon, and water. Cook over low heat until tiny bubbles form around the edges. Remove from the heat and beat the mixture vigorously with a *molinillo* or whisk. Serve at once. *Serves 2.*

Ancient Mexicans displaying crops and livestock (including turkey) at market.

"*In the Days of Plenty,*" *a painting by Quincy Tahoma.*

CHAPTER FIVE

Indian Harvest Festivals: North America

We return thanks to our mother, the earth, which sustains us. We return thanks to the rivers and streams, which supply us with water. We return thanks to all herbs, which furnish medicines for the cure of our diseases. We return thanks to the corn, and to her sisters, the beans and squashes, which give us life. We return thanks to the bushes and trees, which provide us with fruit. We return thanks to the wind, which, moving the air, has banished diseases. We return thanks to the moon and stars, which have given to us their light when the sun was gone. We return thanks to our grandfather He'-no, that he has protected his grandchildren from witches and reptiles, and has given to us his rain. We return thanks to the sun, that he has looked upon the earth with a beneficent eye. Lastly, we return thanks to the Great Spirit, in whom is embodied all goodness, and who directs all things for the good of his children.

—Iroquois address of thanksgiving
to the Great Spirit

THE Mayans and the Aztecs traded seed corn to nearby tribes, who later traded it to other neighbors. In time the art of cultivating corn reached the Indians of North America.

An Iroquois mask made from braided corn husks.

It seems remarkable that a vegetable from the steaming jungles of Central America could also be raised on the New England coast, where the growing season is short and the winters are icy. But corn is a highly adaptable plant.

Through trial and error, the Indians learned to grow varieties that did well in different soils and climates. Some grew so fast that it was possible to raise two crops each year.

Different kinds of corn varied greatly in size. One variety had ears less than an inch long.

Corn of different colors was grown, too. There were blue, red, yellow, white, black, and multi-colored varieties. The Indians of the southwestern United States considered blue corn the most delicious. One of their favorite recipes was blue wafer bread—a thin corncake quickly fried on a hot stone and then rolled into layers.

To preserve the purity of a strain, its seeds were kept carefully separated from other corn seed. When mixed strains did appear, farmers believed that they must have offended the gods, who in revenge had stolen their seeds and substituted others.

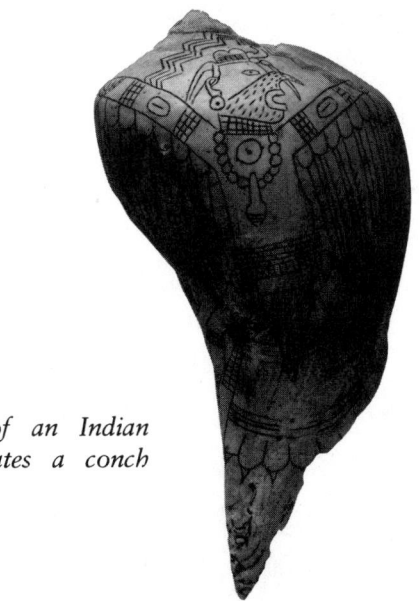

A drawing of an Indian dancer decorates a conch shell.

Most North American Indians had three major corn ceremonies: a planting ceremony, a harvest ceremony, and a green corn ceremony. The last of these was the most important. Its purposes were to give thanks for this year's creation of food and to ask the same blessing for the coming year.

The green corn ceremony was held when the ears of corn were nearly ripe, several weeks before the main harvest. Until this time, the people considered it a crime against the gods to eat, or even to touch, the new corn.

The Creek Indians' "Busk"—the word is from the Creek *boskita,* meaning "to fast"—was an especially interesting green corn ceremony. It marked the end of the old year and the beginning of the new. Though it centered on the renewal of corn, its larger purpose was nothing less than the rebirth of the entire world.

To prepare for the Busk, the Creeks made new clothes and new furniture. Then they built a huge bonfire and burned up their old clothes and furniture, as well as any leftover corn. All other fires in the village were put out. People lit new ones from the Busk bonfire. Foods from the new harvest were cooked in the bonfire and offered to the gods.

"Women Playing Ball on the Prairie," a 19th century painting by Seth Eastman.

This scene of young Indians playing various sports was painted by the first European artist to visit North America, Jacques Le Moyne de Morgues.

After fasting, the Creeks feasted on green corn and venison seasoned with bear oil. The young men played ritual ball games. When it grew dark, they danced in the firelight.

Some tribes not only fasted but also drank a purgative at the start of the ceremony. They wanted to clean out their bodies before they ate the new corn, which they believed contained a divine spirit. This spirit must not be permitted to touch any common, unpurified food when it entered their stomachs.

The Seminole Indians of Florida, for instance, drank a purgative that they called "The Black Drink" the evening before their ceremony. It made them very sick. After they

A Pueblo Indian painting of a Sun Kachina, representing the Spirit of the Sun.

had recovered, they ate new corn (nothing else), and then they fasted. The ceremony concluded with a feast of meat, pumpkins, beans, and berries.

The Pueblo Indians believed that, once upon a time, people ate only meat. But then the rain gods caused a terrible drought. The forests dried up, and the animals died. Finally, Mother Earth took pity on the Pueblos. She told their medicine men to put six pebbles of different colors into a hole and seal it with a large stone. After praying and dancing for four weeks, they were to remove the stone.

They did as Mother Earth had instructed them—and in the hole they found six corn plants. They planted them in six different fields, and each produced corn of a different color. Forever after, the Pueblos raised different-colored corn in different fields.

For their green corn ceremony, the Pueblos performed ritual dances. Among the dancers were the *Koshare*, members of a society that represented the spirits of Pueblo ancestors. The Pueblos believed that their ancestors' spirits could influence the gods on the people's behalf, and that they could communicate with these spirits through dancing.

The Koshare danced with banners attached to long poles. To assure a successful harvest, each person tried to pass under one of the banners at least four times. After the dancing, the people feasted on the new green corn.

The main harvest came weeks later, when the corn in the fields was fully ripe. Before bringing it in, the people carefully cleaned their village. With this gesture of honor and welcome, the Pueblos hoped to persuade the gods to give them good harvests in the future.

Cherokee Indians credited their crops to a spirit called "The Old Woman of the Corn." Her name came from a legend that corn sprang from the blood of an old woman who had been killed by her sons.

The night before they planted their corn, the Cherokees danced around a large grinding bowl. They pretended to pour corn from a basket in one hand into a bowl in the other. This was yet another kind of imitative magic. They were hoping that their acting would encourage the growth of real corn.

When the time came for their green corn ceremony, the high chief sent messages to each of the seven Cherokee towns, inviting them to a feast. Each town signaled its acceptance of the invitation by sending back an ear of green corn—the first one picked.

On the day of the feast, the high chief burned the new ears of corn on a new fire and offered thanks for the har-

Indians sharing a meal of corn and meat. A painting by 16th century explorer John White.

vest to the Old Woman of the Corn. Then the people of the seven towns ate deer meat and green corn.

Weeks later, when the fields of corn were ripe, Cherokee medicine men went to the four corners of each field and wept loudly, much as the ancient Egyptians pretended sorrow at their harvest. This may have been an apology to the Old Woman for cutting the corn and killing its spirit.

Finally, after the corn was harvested in September, the Cherokees held a *ripe* corn ceremony. Again the people of the seven towns came together to dance and to pray and to feast on corn, beans, pumpkins, and wild turkey.

The Iroquois Indians held a green corn ceremony called *ah-dake-wao*, which means simply "a feast." Ah-dake-wao lasted four days. The people prayed, danced, played games, and sang songs of thanksgiving. At the end of each day they feasted on large helpings of succotash stew.

The Iroquois also had ceremonies to honor the ripening of different kinds of berries: blackberries, raspberries, cranberries (thought to be good for the liver and blood), blueberries, elderberries, and huckleberries. But it was strawberries, which they called "The First Fruit of the Earth," that they loved best, and it was the strawberry festival that was most important.

The women gathered the ripe strawberries in June. The chief began the festival with a prayer of thanksgiving. Then he sprinkled grains of tobacco over a fire, because the Iroquois believed that tobacco smoke was pleasing to the gods. As the smoke curled upward, they sang, danced, and played games: darts and lacrosse were especially popular. The festival ended with a feast of strawberries, sweetened with maple syrup and cooked with a topping of corn pudding.

A portrait of the famous Seneca chief, Cornplanter.

Even some tribes that did no farming, but lived by gathering wild fruit or digging the roots of wild plants, held harvest festivals when their favorite foods were in season.

For instance, the Salish Indians were especially fond of wild raspberries. The young berries were cooked in a new pot over a new fire. The Salish stood in a circle around the fire with their eyes closed, and their chief called to the spirit of the raspberry plant, begging it for good harvests. Later, the cooked berries were passed from hand to hand in a newly carved wooden dish. Everyone ate his portion with reverence, for the Salish believed that the berries contained the spirit to which their chief had just prayed.

And not every harvest was a harvest of fruits or vegetables. The Karok Indians of California depended upon their catch of salmon. They held a ceremony each year when the salmon began to run, imploring the gods to grant them good fishing.

GUS-GA'-A
THE PEACHSTONE GAME

This game of chance was sometimes played at the end of the green corn ceremony. The Indians probably taught it to the early colonists, and it may even have been played at the Pilgrims' first Thanksgiving.

Rules: Use four clean, dry peachstones. Paint one side of each stone yellow, and the other side blue. (Or whatever two colors you choose.) Give each color a number value. For example, let yellow equal two, and blue equal four.

Each player takes a turn shaking the peachstones in a bowl. When he sets the bowl down, his score is found by adding the number values of the colors that are facing up. The player with the highest score is the winner.

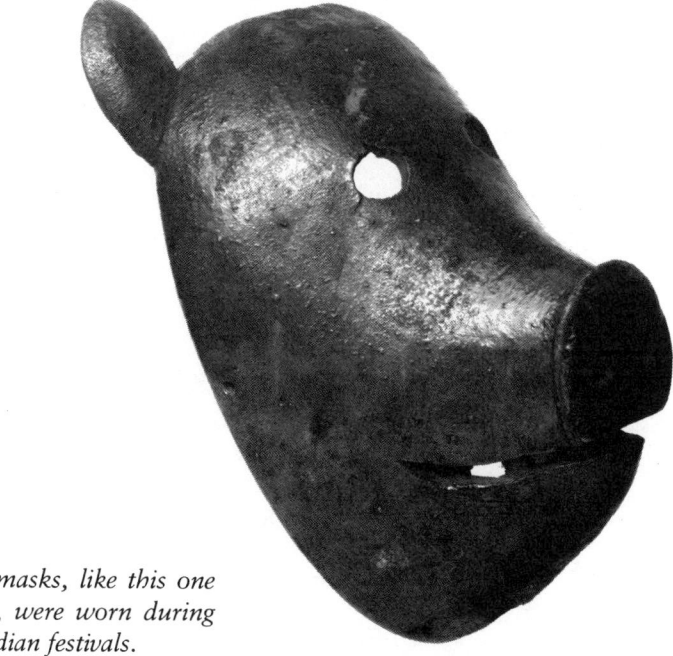

Animal masks, like this one of a pig, were worn during many Indian festivals.

IROQUOIS SUCCOTASH

An original Iroquois recipe directs the cook to "cut corn kernels off the cob with a deer's jaw" and to "flavor the succotash with bear's flesh." Here's an adaptation that uses modern methods and stew meat to make a complete supper in a dish.

1½ cups fresh lima beans   *3 tablespoons butter*
1½ cups fresh corn kernels   *2 tablespoons cream*
1 pound stew meat, diced in   *salt and pepper*
* small pieces*

Bring ¼ cup of water to a boil. Add the fresh lima beans and return to a boil. Cover, reduce the heat, and simmer until tender, about 30 minutes. Drain.

Bring 2 tablespoons of water to a boil. Add the fresh corn and return to a boil. Cover, reduce the heat, and simmer until tender, 2 to 5 minutes. Drain.

Melt the butter. Add the stew meat and brown on all sides over medium heat. Sprinkle with salt and pepper. Stir the cooked lima beans and corn into the meat. Add the cream.

Mix the cornstarch with ¼ cup water, stirring until the mixture is smooth. Add to the meat and stir gently until the sauce thickens, about 3 minutes. Serve at once.   *Serves 4.*

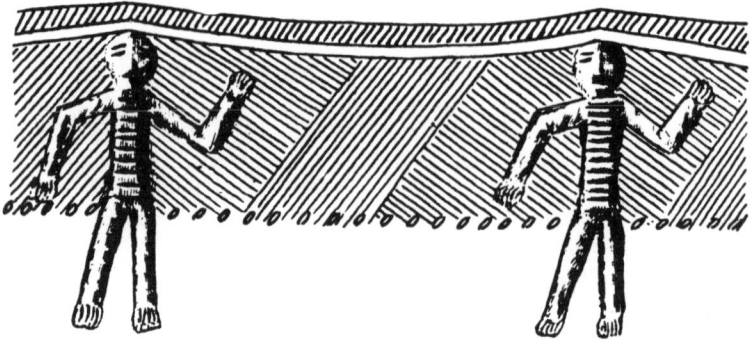

An Iroquois pottery design.

CHAPTER SIX

The Pilgrims

Heap high the board with plenteous cheer,
and gather to the feast,
And toast the sturdy Pilgrim band whose
courage never ceased.

—ALICE WILLIAMS BROTHERTON,
"The First Thanksgiving"

COLONIAL AMERICANS, if they were to survive in a new and strange wilderness, needed enterprise and determination—the same qualities that would later win their nation's independence. Their earliest reward was the first Thanksgiving, in October of 1621. The small band of immigrants who gathered then at Plymouth, Massachusetts, have become a symbol of brave, hard-working colonial America. The more we know of their story, the more remarkable their achievement seems.

Religion was the wind and tide that brought them to America. They had lived in England at a time when religious freedom was restricted, and they could not worship as they chose. They therefore decided to become *pilgrims*—people who travel to a distant place in order to worship there.

But their first destination was not America. In 1609, a group of about a hundred pilgrims fled from England to a nation famous for religious freedom: Holland, the land of the Dutch. Holland was one of the nearest nations of Europe, with which England had had commercial ties for centuries—no wilderness, but still a strange and foreign place.

The Pilgrims settled in the city of Leyden, a center of the Dutch clothing industry and the site of an important university. The Dutch had built the university a few years before to celebrate a military victory over Spain. Spain and Holland were still enemies, though, and the Pilgrims worried about a possible Spanish invasion. Spain allowed even less religious freedom than England did.

Still, for now the Pilgrims were safe. The Dutch permitted them to have their own meeting hall and their own minister. Some of the Pilgrims became weavers, tailors,

Delft Haven, Holland, where the Pilgrims began their journey to the New World.

Elaborate earring designs from 17th century Holland.

ribbon makers, button makers, carders and combers of wool. Others worked as masons and bricklayers.

But, for people who had come from farms, such jobs were strange and difficult. And life among foreigners never became comfortable. As the years passed, the Pilgrims grew worried. Their children spoke Dutch as though it were their own language. Were they also becoming attached to the Dutch way of life? Although the Pilgrims were grateful to their easy-going hosts, they also disapproved of what they considered Dutch frivolousness, and considered it a threat to their children's education and morality.

So at last they decided they must undertake another journey, far longer and more dangerous, to a place where they would be not guests but pioneers—to the American wilderness.

They were financed by a group of English investors, the Merchant Adventurers. It was agreed that the Pilgrims would work for their backers for seven years. During that time they would not even own their houses. Any profits their labor earned would be divided among the shareholders of the Merchant Adventurers. In return, the Pilgrims got passage to the New World, and supplies to maintain them for the first hard months.

Only forty-four of them finally went. Some were too old or too young to bear the hardships they would face. Still others withdrew at the last minute out of an understandable fear. Those who went hoped to be able to send later for those who stayed behind.

Along with the Pilgrims, the Merchant Adventurers sent sixty-six other people. These were called "Strangers" to distinguish them from the Pilgrim "Saints."

The group sailed from Plymouth, England, on September 6, 1620. Their ship, the Mayflower, was small, crowded, and leaky. Everyone aboard—Saints, Strangers, and crew—spent much of the journey soaked to the skin with the salt water of the cold Atlantic. There were fierce storms, one of which cracked a mast. By what must have seemed a miracle, someone had brought a huge iron screw from Holland. The sailors were able to use it to repair the mast.

A ship much like the Mayflower.

Even though everything was always damp, the danger of fire aboard ship meant that cooking was rarely permitted. Almost all food was eaten cold.

The diet was monotonous. There were dried peas and moldy cheese. There were biscuits—a simple mixture of flour and water baked so long that it was almost too hard to bite into. Nevertheless the biscuits soon became infested with weevils that tunneled through the rocky lumps.

There was beef preserved in salt. Because grains of salt were called "corns," this was known as "corned beef." When corned beef was eaten, the excess salt was supposed to be soaked out with fresh water to make the beef palatable. But the Mayflower didn't carry enough water for this purpose. The voyagers drank beer.

The crossing must have been difficult enough even for the sailors, but still more so for the inexperienced and ill-prepared passengers. It took sixty-five days. One passenger died, many were sick, and even the healthy became weak. At last, on November 10, they caught their first glimpse of land—Cape Cod.

But now arguments sprang up. The sailors, who wanted to return to England at once, demanded that the captain set the passengers ashore immediately. And the Strangers declared their intention of starting a separate settlement of their own. This was grim news to the Pilgrims. Many other small settlements had failed, and they doubted that theirs could survive unless the two groups stayed together.

So a meeting was held aboard ship, at which the Saints and Strangers talked about their disagreements and how to resolve them. Finally they drafted the famous Mayflower Compact, setting forth how their shared settlement would be governed. The two groups became so unified that from this point on they are all called "Pilgrims."

Only men signed the Mayflower Compact. Though women had some legal rights, government was in the hands of their husbands. Nevertheless, the Mayflower Compact was an important and valuable document, promising "just and equall lawes" for all. It stated that the settlers would choose their own governor—they chose John Carver as their first—and could, if they wished, replace him. This was truly the beginning of democratic government in America.

But there was still the immediate problem of how to stay alive. Delay in setting sail had cost them several months. It was already too late in the season to plant crops. The colonists would have to shoot game, gather wild plants, and live off the ship's dwindling provisions until spring. Luckily the Captain of the Mayflower, Master Christopher Jones, persuaded his crew to stay on through the winter, so the settlers could use the ship as a base while they started building their new homes.

The Orthodox true Minifter, the Seducer and falfe Prophet.

A book published in 1648 shows a popular view of groups like the Pilgrims, who disagreed with the Church of England.

The Pilgrims landing at Plymouth, as pictured by a 19th century artist.

Choosing a location for the settlement was not easy. A group of men went exploring along the shore. They saw some Indians and tried to catch up with them, but the Indians disappeared into the forest.

Then the Englishmen came upon a mound of sand beside an abandoned Indian cornfield. Digging into the mound, they found baskets of yellow, blue, and red seed corn that the Indians had buried. Resolving to repay the Indians—which they eventually did—they carried it back to the ship to plant when spring came.

A few days later, a party of men went exploring along the coast in a small sailboat that they had brought along on the Mayflower. When they came to Plymouth, which had been named by Captain John Smith in 1614, they decided that they had found the perfect place.

There was an excellent harbor. There were even several fields that had already been cleared by Indians. There was a large brook, providing fish and fresh water. A steep hill offered a good place to build a fort that could be easily defended. The Pilgrims' greatest fear was a swift attack by the Indians. Weakened as many of them were, they could scarcely have defended themselves. They didn't know that the local Indians, predominantly Patuxets, were peaceful. Nor did they know that, only three years earlier, most of these Indians had been wiped out by a terrible disease— possibly bubonic plague, brought from Europe by early explorers. The Pilgrims were surprised when not a single Indian appeared during the first winter.

On Christmas Day, 1620, they started work on their settlement. The cold was intense. Workers were blasted by snow and sleet. Almost immediately, many people became ill. William Bradford, later to become the colony's governor, called it the time of the "Great Sickness."

Sometimes several people died in a day. They were buried secretly, at night, in unmarked graves, so that any Indians who might be watching would not know how few settlers were left. Of the 110 who had set sail from England, fewer than 50 survived that first winter.

Those who were healthy, often only six or seven at a time, worked on construction and nursed the others. And in March, when the weather finally improved, so did the settlers' health.

Still, they were barely able to gather enough food to keep from starving. They were inexperienced at stalking game. They hadn't brought with them the right kind of fishhooks or traps. Whatever they caught or found that was edible, they ate. Once they ate an eagle, and decided that it tasted like mutton.

Even when their food seemed adequate in sheer bulk, fueling their bodies proved strangely difficult. In England and Holland, their diet had been largely based on grain, and was therefore high in calories—as many as 6,000 calories per person per day. Their American diet of roots and fish and lean, stringy wildfowl simply wasn't as satisfying as the puddings and breads and beer that had been their staple foods in Europe.

So they were eager to plant crops as soon as the weather permitted—English barley and wheat and peas, and Indian corn. They moved their belongings off the Mayflower and crowded into the few small houses they had built. Single men had to live with families. Nobody had much privacy, but at least everyone had shelter.

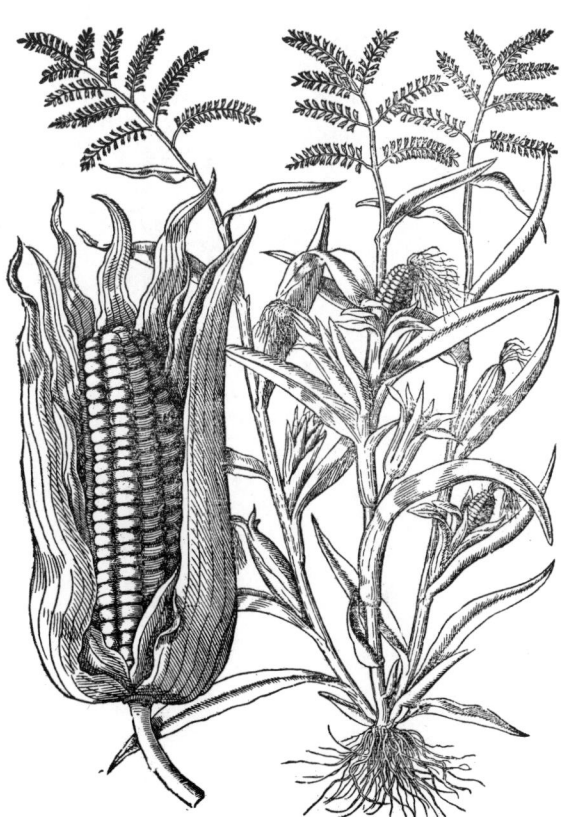

The manner of their attire and painting them selues when they goe to their generall huntings or at theire Solemne feasts.

Sixteenth century explorer John White's painting of an Indian clothed and decorated for a feast or a hunt.

CHAPTER SEVEN

Squanto and Massasoit

THAT SPRING—on March 16, 1621—something important and startling happened. An Indian brave appeared in Plymouth settlement. He walked along the main
street toward the Common House. The frightened settlers
were about to rush for their guns when he suddenly called
out "Welcome"—*in English*.

His name was Samoset, and he was an Abnaki Indian.
He had learned a little English, he explained, from the
captains of fishing boats that sailed off the coast of Newfoundland. And he told them about Massasoit (which means
"Big Chief"), a Wampanoag Indian who lived about forty
miles from Plymouth and who wanted to meet the settlers'
leaders.

Samoset stayed in Plymouth that night and left the next
day. Soon he reappeared with another Indian called Tis-
quantum, or Squanto. Squanto spoke even better English

than his friend. He told the settlers his astonishing story. Squanto had already been back and forth across the ocean to England three times!

The first time, he and four other Indians had been captured by Captain George Waymouth. Captain Waymouth took him across the ocean to Plymouth, England, to the home of Waymouth's employer—a rich investor, Sir Fernando Gorges.

It was Gorges who had taught Squanto to speak English. He wanted to get information of commercial value from Squanto—what the climate was like, which crops grew best along the coast, what kind of game was to be found, where the fishing grounds were richest, which Indian tribes were peaceful and which were warlike. Armed with such information, Sir Fernando hoped to make profitable investments in the New World.

When Captain John Smith sailed for America in 1614, Squanto sailed back with him. Smith was working for

In the 1620's, when this drawing was made, Indians and settlers were just beginning to live together in North America.

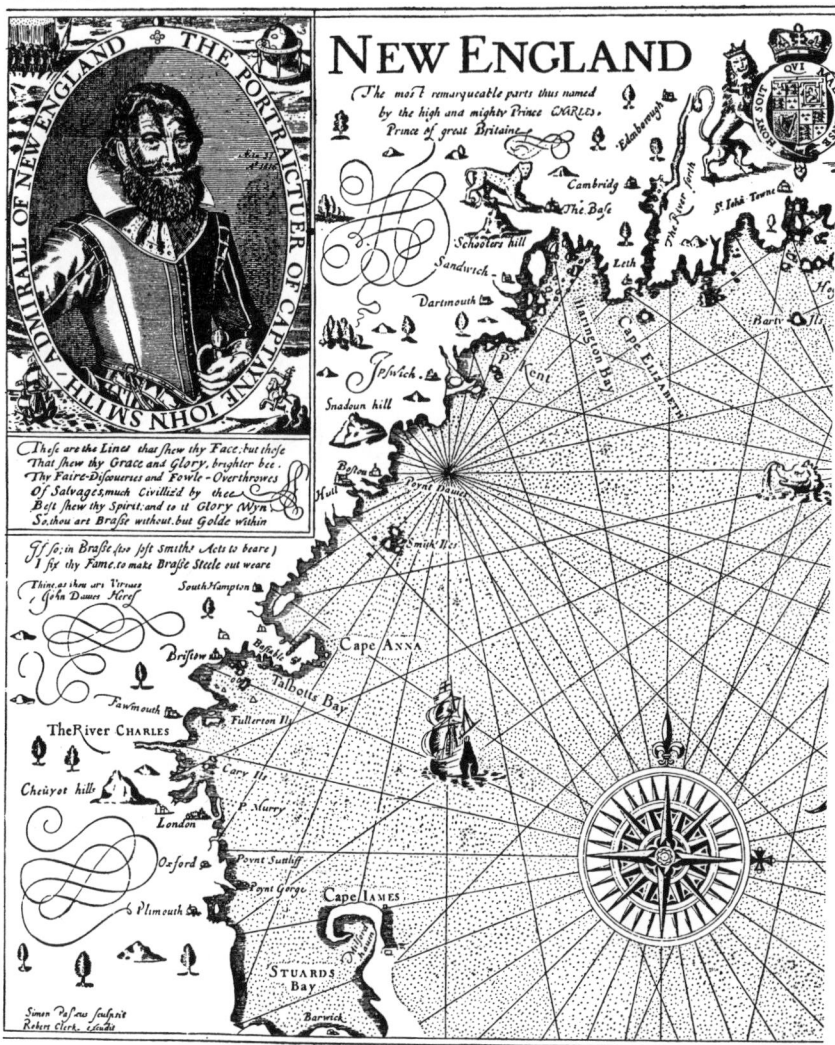

Captain John Smith's map of New England, 1614.

backers who expected him to hunt for whales and gold, but he decided to search for furs and fish instead. Squanto helped Smith barter with the Indians. Then he went home to his people at Patuxet.

But there, after only a few weeks of freedom, he was captured by *another* Englishman, Captain Thomas Hunt. Captain Hunt took him, along with twenty other captured Indians, to Spain, where he sold most of them into slavery. The rest, including Squanto, were seized by an order of Spanish friars who wanted to convert the Indians to Christianity.

Squanto managed to escape and find his way to England. There he sought help from Master John Slany of Cornhill. Slany was a merchant who arranged expeditions to the New World, and he found a place for Squanto on a ship that was sailing to Newfoundland.

In Newfoundland, Squanto met Captain Dermer, a representative of the same Sir Fernando Gorges whom Squanto had known in England. Captain Dermer was looking for the best site to found a new colony. Squanto, who was anxious to get home, convinced him that the site should be Patuxet. But Dermer insisted that they first return to England and get permission from Sir Fernando. So once again Squanto made the long, uncomfortable trip back and forth across the ocean.

Finally they arrived in New England. But as they sailed down the coast they made a horrible discovery: almost all the Indians had been wiped out by a plague. Villages were crumbling, crops rotting, and the few survivors almost too weak to take care of themselves. Squanto's own tribe had been completely destroyed.

So Squanto went to stay with the great chief Massasoit at Narragansett Bay. A year later, Samoset arrived with news of the Pilgrims, and Squanto returned with him to Plymouth.

Squanto's importance to the Pilgrims was enormous. In fact, it is not certain that their colony could have survived without his help. William Bradford wrote that Squanto was "a speciall instrumente sent of God for their good beyond their expectation."

To begin with, he helped arrange a meeting between

the pilgrims and Chief Massasoit. On March 22, 1621, the Chief arrived in Plymouth with 60 Wampanoag braves. His face was painted. His hair was coated with bear grease. He wore a squirrel-skin coat and beads of bone. He carried a knife and a tomahawk.

The Pilgrims, undoubtedly impressed, decided in turn to impress the Indians. Governor John Carver made his appearance to the roll of drums and blare of trumpets. He told Massasoit that the great English ruler, King James, sent him messages of love and peace. Massasoit was escorted to a house furnished with a rug and cushions. Here the Pilgrims and Indians toasted their friendship with brandy.

Then they negotiated a treaty, in which the Pilgrims and the Wampanoags agreed to live in peace. The Indians would return some farming tools that they had taken, and the Pilgrims would pay for the seed corn that they had taken

The signatures of some of the Pilgrims, including leaders William Bradford, William Brewster, and Myles Standish.

when they first arrived. Each group would punish any of
its people who harmed a member of the other group. When
they visited each other, they would always come un-
armed. Finally, each group would come to the other's aid
in case of attack by a third party.

*The Pilgrims, anxious to avoid trouble with the Indians, made a point of
showing off their firearms—like the musket carried by this soldier of the
early 1600's.*

This treaty was fair to both sides, which may explain why it lasted for 50 years.

It was valuable to the Wampanoags because the plague that had killed most of their people had left them vulnerable to attack by their neighbors to the west, the bellicose Narragansetts and Pequots. The Pilgrims, with their amazing guns and cannons, were powerful allies.

The Pilgrims needed help just as badly. They were few in number, unfamiliar with the trackless forests, and didn't understand Indian methods of warfare. Just as the Mayflower Compact permitted the founding of Plymouth Colony, the treaty with the Wampanoags permitted the colony's survival.

After the treaty was negotiated, Massasoit and his braves left. But Squanto stayed with the Pilgrims throughout the spring, teaching them many lessons about survival in the American wilderness.

He taught them how to tap maple trees for the sugary sap. He taught them how to dig eels from the mud at low tide. He showed them which plants were poisonous and which had medicinal powers.

Most important by far, he taught them how to plant Indian corn. Other English colonies had been starved out when they tried to grow crops as they had at home: by "broadcasting" the seed—simply casting it about them—and covering it loosely with soil. In America, this didn't work.

Squanto taught the Pilgrims how to work the earth with the shells of quahogs (a kind of clam). The Indian technique, which the Pilgrims now learned, was to heap the earth in low mounds three or four feet apart. In each mound, several seeds were buried, together with—no doubt to the Pilgrims' surprise—an equal number of fish.

The idea, and it worked very well, was that the rotting fish fertilized the sprouting corn. During the planting season—"when the elm leaves are the size of a squirrel's ear"—fish were plentiful. Herrings and alewives were making their spring run up the brooks.

Other vegetables were often planted together with corn. Beans went right in the same hole, so that their vines grew up the cornstalks, and pumpkins and squash were planted in between the mounds.

Finally, Squanto explained to the Pilgrims that they should set a guard in the cornfields every night, to keep away the wolves. Wolves—which at that time ranged everywhere in North America—were attracted by the smell of the fish, and liked to dig up the mounds.

In later years, when the Pilgrims kept dogs, wolves were less likely to approach. But the dogs liked to dig up the mounds, too! The Pilgrims had to tie the dogs' forepaws at planting time.

The corn that the Pilgrims grew was different in appearance and texture from our corn. The cobs were smaller. The kernels were red, yellow, blue, black, or even a mixture of colors. The Pilgrims sometimes roasted it on the cob, sometimes dried and preserved it, and sometimes soaked off the hulls and cooked the soft inner kernels in stews, puddings, and bread. Except that they did not have such specialties as cornflakes, the Pilgrims—like the Indians for hundreds of years before them—ate corn in all the ways that we eat it today.

This painting by John White shows an Indian woman holding a basket of ground corn.

"God be praised," Edward Winslow wrote, "we had a good increase of Indian corn."

By the time of the harvest, in October, the Pilgrims had reason to feel optimistic about their future. They were at peace with their Indian neighbors. They had enough buildings to shelter them through the winter. They were healthy. And they had, all of a sudden, plenty to eat.

True, the barley and peas that they had planted from English seeds had done poorly. But there were good crops of beans and squash. And the yield of corn, as Edward Winslow wrote, was enormous. The Pilgrims calculated that there was enough to provide each person with two pounds of corn meal per day.

So it was natural that, after they had put away their food for winter—the corn shucked and stored in corn-cribs, the fruits and vegetables dried, the fish packed in salt, the meat cured over smoky fires—the Pilgrims de-cided to celebrate. In Edward Winslow's words:

> Our harvest being gotten in, our governor sent four men on fowling, that so we might after a special man-ner rejoice together after we had gathered the fruit of our labors. They four in one day killed as much fowl as, with a little help beside, served the company al-most a week.

But the fowl alone was not nearly enough, for the number of celebrators turned out to be much greater than the Pil-grims expected. Continuing Winslow's account:

> Many of the Indians [came] amongst us, and among the rest their greatest king Massasoit, with some ninety men, whom for three days we entertained and feasted.

Squanto had been sent to invite Massasoit. But when the chief accepted, he brought 90 braves with him! The Pilgrims were appalled. All these guests had, of course, to be fed generously. But to do that would mean using up the supplies that they needed to survive the winter. For-tunately, Massasoit himself took care of the problem. He sent some of his men into the forest to hunt, and they soon returned with five deer.

Thus began the first Thanksgiving. It lasted for several days, perhaps as long as a week. We have no record of just

The seething of in Potts *their meate of earth.*

Some of the food for the Pilgrims' Thanksgiving was probably cooked in clay pots over an open fire. A 16th century watercolor by John White.

what the Pilgrims ate. But the four men who were sent out to shoot fowl may have returned with wild ducks and geese. (In England, goose had been the traditional holiday feast.) Was there turkey as well? Unfortunately we shall never know.

The Indian's deer meat was a luxury to the Pilgrims. In England, deer had been eaten only by the very rich, who kept them in private parks. The Pilgrims cooked some of the deer meat in cornmeal "pasties"—a kind of meat pie. The rest was cooked in the same way as the fowl: on long spits that women and children turned over the fire.

Whole ears of corn were roasted directly in the fire, and cornbread wrapped in leaves was cooked the same way.

The first Thanksgiving, as imagined by artist Doris Lee.

There was probably fish, baked in earth ovens, or simmered in chowders and stews. Local fish and shellfish included eels, lobsters, mussels, clams, oysters, cod, and salmon.

And there were certainly puddings. As a substitute for frumenty, the wheat pudding that was featured at English harvest celebrations, the Pilgrims probably boiled cornmeal and water to make *hasty pudding*. This they flavored with grapes, berries, and perhaps maple syrup. We don't know how hasty pudding got its name. Mixing up the ingredients may have been a quick job, but they took a very long time to cook.

Another early pudding, which the Pilgrims could have invented on the spot, was pumpkin pudding. It became a staple of the New England diet. Eventually, sweetened with molasses or maple sugar and baked in a crust, it evolved into a traditional Thanksgiving favorite—pumpkin pie.

The first Thanksgiving may also have included a food that we do *not* associate with the holiday: popcorn! We know that many Indian tribes had learned that corn could be popped. According to an old story, one of the Pilgrims' guests—Quadequina, Massasoit's brother—went into the woods and returned with a deerskin full of popped corn. If the story is true, the Pilgrims must have been amazed and delighted. And it is certainly true that popcorn became a great favorite in New England, so much so that the colonists often ate it for breakfast with a bit of milk or cream.

The Pilgrims played games brought over from England.

English feasts usually ended with wheatcakes and ale. But the Pilgrims had no wheat. We can guess that, as a substitute, they made thick little cakes of cornmeal and cooked them, Indian style, on hot stones. The cakes would have resembled dry, crumbly pancakes.

Artists' portrayals of the first Thanksgiving usually show Pilgrims and Indians eating together at long tables. But in fact they probably sat on the ground. The Pilgrims didn't have nearly enough tables and chairs for everyone. People probably helped themselves to whatever they wanted whenever they felt hungry, throughout the several days of the feast. They ate with their fingers, or speared food on knives. Some may have ladeled it onto trenchers—rough plates made of wood or stale bread.

When the eating was finally done, the Pilgrims ran races and played games. They gave a military show: marching, playing drums and bugles, firing their muskets. The Indians demonstrated their skills with the bow and arrow.

This must have been a time of happiness and rejoicing for the Pilgrims. Against great odds they had built homes in the wilderness, raised enough crops to keep themselves alive during the coming winter, and arranged a treaty of friendship with the Indians. This was truly a time for thanksgiving.

Here are three old English games that may have been played at the first Thanksgiving.

THE STAGGIN MATCH

"Two folks with feet tied together and wrists tied behind shall seek to knock one-an-other over. No butting."

A EGGE RACE TO BE RUNN

"Every person runs to the goal and back with an egg held full in the mouth. First person to cross over the finish line with the egge in mouth unbroken winneth."

A JINGLYNG MATCH

"Several folks with blindfolds try to catch the bellringer. The first contestor to tag him wins, yet if the ringer eludeth all for the appointed time, he then taketh the prize. No unwynking.*

*peeking

CHAPTER EIGHT

How Thanksgiving Grew

The Old Wives' Program for
Thanksgiving Week:
MONDAY—Wash
TUESDAY—Scour
WEDNESDAY—Bake
THURSDAY—Devour!

—MOTHER GOOSE

T HE FAMOUS Pilgrim celebration at Plymouth Colony, Massachusetts, in 1621 is traditionally regarded as the first American Thanksgiving. But at least two other states claim earlier Thanksgivings.

On December 14, 1619—two years before the feast at Plymouth—there was a celebration in Virginia. This was purely a religious observance, not a meal. Captain John Woodleaf led 39 colonists many miles up the James River from Jamestown. At a place called Berkeley Hundred they went ashore and gave thanks for their safe arrival.

Captain Woodleaf proclaimed that the ceremony would

Nova Britannia.

OFFERING MOST

Excellent fruites by Planting in VIRGINIA.

Exciting all such as be well affected to further the same.

LONDON
Printed for Samvel Macham, and are to be sold at his Shop in Pauls Church-yard, at the Signe of the Bul-head.
1609.

Settlers were attracted to the New World by appeals like this one, printed in 1609.

be held every year. "Wee ordaine," he wrote, "that the day of our ships arrivall at the place assigned for plantacon in the land of Virginia shall be yearly and perpetualy keept holy as a day of thanksgiving to Almighty God."

But the settlers at Berkeley Hundred were not able to keep Captain Woodleaf's vow. A few years later they were all killed by Indians.

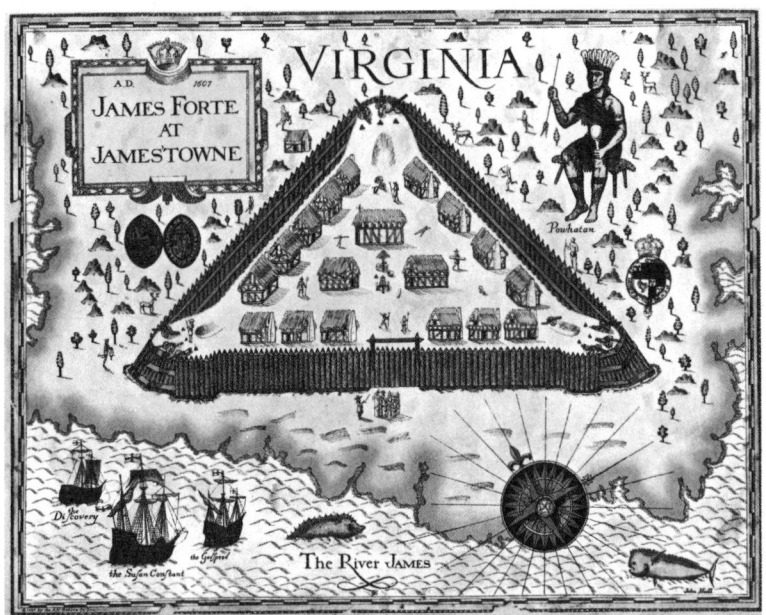

An early Virginia settlement.

Maine claims an even earlier Thanksgiving. Fourteen years before the ceremony at Plymouth, English settlers, led by Captain George Popham, met with Abnaki Indians near the mouth of the Kennebec River to share a harvest feast and prayer meeting.

But like the ceremony in Virginia, the Maine Thanksgiving was never repeated. Popham's colony failed, and the settlers returned to England the following spring.

Plymouth was different. It became a permanent settlement. That is why the Plymouth Pilgrims have become the symbol of the American Thanksgiving.

But where did the Pilgrims get the idea of doing such a thing? Just as they had brought fishhooks and guns and seeds and farming tools from England, so had they brought their English traditions. And in England, as we have seen, they had celebrated a form of Thanksgiving called Harvest Home.

During the ten years they lived in the city of Leyden, the Pilgrims were probably also influenced by Dutch traditions. The Dutch held many "fast-prayer and thank days."

And the citizens of Leyden had a special thanksgiving ceremony that was all their own. Once, when Holland and Spain were at war, Leyden had been besieged by Spanish troops. For five months, no food or supplies entered the city.

The citizens were exhausted and starving by the time Dutch soldiers drove away the Spanish on October 3, 1574. They hungrily devoured the first supplies of food brought in: raw herring, bread, carrots, onions, and potatoes.

And every year after that, to give thanks on the anniversary of their liberation, the people of Leyden ate herring, bread, and *hodepodge* (a stew of carrots, onions, potatoes, and whatever meat or poultry was available). They danced, played games, and set off fireworks.

In America, the Pilgrims' practices greatly resembled those customary in England and those they had observed among the Dutch. In bad times they fasted, to honor God and strengthen their spirits. In good times they gave thanks.

The Pilgrims' ceremonial days varied greatly from year to year. Sometimes their thanksgiving observances fell during the Harvest Home feast that they had known in England.

Other days of thanksgiving were purely religious occasions, entirely separate from any celebration of the harvest. These might occur at any time.

In 1623, for example, Plymouth Colony was suffering a severe drought. The crops were dying. If rain failed to come, the Pilgrims would starve. William Bradford, their Governor, proclaimed a day of fasting and prayer.

And at sunset the Pilgrims were overjoyed to see clouds appear in the sky. That night, as one of them recorded, there came "a long, refreshing rain." The crops were saved. To show their gratitude to God, the Pilgrims set aside a special day for thanksgiving prayer.

Dates for thanksgiving remained variable through the eighteenth century. For instance, in 1705 the town of Colchester, Connecticut, postponed its thanksgiving ceremony because of a delay in the arrival of molasses—necessary for many holiday pies and puddings.

During the Revolutionary War, the Continental Congress appointed several thanksgiving days to celebrate victories over the British. And in 1784, after the war was won,

The state seal of Connecticut.

the Congress proclaimed a day to give thanks for the return of peace. George Washington, our first president, named November 26, 1789, as a day of thanksgiving to honor the adoption of the Constitution.

For decades, the governors of the various states proclaimed Thanksgiving irregularly—or not at all. It was most popular in New England. But by the early nineteenth century, most of the Mid-Atlantic states were celebrating it too.

The South, by contrast, was slow to adopt the custom. This was partly a matter of regional rivalry. Many Southerners associated Thanksgiving with what they considered New England bigotry. But finally, in 1855, Virginia proclaimed a day of statewide thanksgiving. Other Southern states soon followed.

There was, however, a growing movement to establish one Thanksgiving day that would be honored everywhere in America. The leader of this movement was Sarah Josepha Hale, founder and editor of *Godey's Lady's Book*, a popular magazine. For nearly forty years she wrote editorials, gave speeches, and sent letters to Presidents, gov-

Fashionable ladies of the 1860's were avid readers of Godey's Lady's Book.

ernors, and members of Congress. Mrs. Hale wanted Thanksgiving to fall on the 4th of July—Independence Day.

Most other people favored a November date, however, and it was their desire that finally prevailed. On November 26, 1863, President Abraham Lincoln formally established America's Thanksgiving on the fourth Thursday in November. Lincoln wrote:

> The year that is drawing to a close has been filled with the blessings of fruitful skies. . . . It has seemed to me fit and proper that they should be solemnly, reverently, and gratefully acknowledged with one heart and one voice by the American people.

He made his proclamation at a crucial point in the Civil War—the Union victory at Gettysburg—and the states of the Confederacy did not recognize Lincoln's authority. Nevertheless, the date was now established, and after the war it came to be observed nationwide.

In 1939, President Franklin Roosevelt moved Thanksgiving from the fourth to the third Thursday in November. He wanted to stimulate the economy by allowing more shopping days between Thanksgiving and Christmas. But by that time the traditional date was so well established that Roosevelt's change created an uproar. In 1941, a joint resolution of Congress reestablished Thanksgiving on the fourth Thursday of November, where it remains today.

DUTCH HODGEPODGE

1 chicken, cut in serving pieces	*2 large potatoes*
3 tablespoons butter	*4 sprigs parsley, chopped*
4 carrots	*1 teaspoon dried marjoram*
3 small leeks	*1 bay leaf*
1 pound small white onions	*1 teaspoon salt*
2 medium turnips	*½ teaspoon ground black pepper*

Melt the butter in a heavy skillet. Add the chicken pieces and cook briefly until golden. Transfer them to a heavy pot.

Wash the vegetables. Peel the carrots and slice them in 2-inch pieces. Cut the leeks in 2-inch pieces. Peel the onions. Peel and quarter the turnips. Quarter the potatoes.

Put the vegetables on top of the chicken. Add the parsley, marjoram, bay leaf, salt, and pepper, and enough cold water to cover the chicken and vegetables. Bring to a boil. Reduce the heat, cover, and simmer 1½ hours. Some of the liquid will boil away. Serve the remaining liquid in soup bowls. Put a piece of chicken and some vegetables in each bowl along with the broth.   *Serves 4–6.*

CHAPTER NINE

Some Special American Thanksgivings

Thanksgiving Day . . . the one that is purely American!

—O. Henry,
"Two Thanksgiving Day Gentlemen"

AMERICANS EVERYWHERE share certain Thanksgiving traditions. But there are also some special and unusual regional ceremonies. Two of these originated in Hawaii and Alaska.

Long before Europeans settled in America, native Hawaiians were celebrating the longest thanksgiving festival in the world—*Makahiki*. Makahiki lasted four months, roughly from November through February—the exact dates depended on the moon and tides. For the rest of the year, the people worked hard. But during Makahiki, both work and war were forbidden.

Makahiki began with the collection of thanks offerings for the king. These offerings served as taxes, but had a religious significance, too. Each village brought its gifts to Lono, the Hawaiian god of plenty—a kind and gentle god

The state seal of Hawaii.

who blessed his people with ample rain and fertile soil.

A huge wooden statue of Lono, sprinkled with coconut oil, decorated with vegetation and feathers, was carried from village to village by a procession of priests. At every stop they collected the offerings that the *Konoliku* (village chief) had gathered from his people. Each village contributed, according to its ability, from the first crops harvested. The villagers also offered Lono pigs, flowers, rare seashells, edible ferns, woven fiber mats, and feathers of the iiwi and mamos birds.

Upon receiving these offerings, the priests prayed to Lono and proclaimed that the land had been made free. The people feasted, sang, and danced the hula. They were told to sleep only on their softest mats, and only when they were too exhausted for more merrymaking.

Sports were an important part of Makahiki, especially racing, boxing, wrestling, spear throwing, and a game of bowls played with stones. War games were conducted, too.

Makahiki concluded—dramatically and dangerously—with the test of spears. The king had to prove himself worthy to continue in his office. Everyone crowded onto the beach, and the king headed out to sea in his special red canoe. When he returned and approached the shore, a group

A view of Hawaii in the 19th century.

of warriors rushed at him with raised spears. If they killed him, a new king was chosen to lead the people. If he managed to get ashore in spite of them he was safe, and led a royal procession that signaled the end of the festival.

The Eskimos of Alaska, where the harsh climate permits very little leisure, could not afford four months of celebration. Their thanksgiving was short and specific, marking the successful harvest of one of their most important foods: whales.

Whale hunts took place in the spring. When the frozen sea ice began to break up, crews of men set out in umiaks—small boats with hulls made from animal hide. The hunt was extremely dangerous, not only because of the whales, but also because the umiaks could be crushed by the gigantic ice floes all around them.

The Alaska state seal.

When they sighted a whale, the hunters tried to spear it with a special retrieving harpoon attached to a long line. Inflated seal skins were tied to the line, placing a drag on the harpooned whale that eventually exhausted it. Then the carcass was towed to shore.

After the hunt, the men dragged their umiaks out of the water and turned them on their sides to make a shelter from the cold ocean wind. Then the festival began. The people feasted on whale meat, danced and sang, and played games.

In one game, the Eskimos used a large piece of walrus hide as a kind of trampoline. The men stood in a circle, holding the hide taut. Then one man jumped onto it and the others tossed him repeatedly into the air—sometimes as high as twenty feet—while he tried to keep his balance and land on his feet. Each man had his turn.

In the evening, everyone danced and sang to the rhythm of a large drum, so large that it was beaten by five men at a time. The drumming, chanting, and dancing lasted late into the night.

An Eskimo drawing.

Another special American thanksgiving has been celebrated in Pennsylvania since colonial times by members of the Schwenkfelder Society.

Like the Pilgrims, the Schwenkfelders came to America in search of religious freedom. Their religious movement—the Reformation of the Middle Way—had developed in the 1500's, based on the writings of a European nobleman named Kaspar Schwenckfeld.

In 1734, after centuries of persecution, 180 Schwenkfelders fled from Silesia (an area now divided among Germany, Poland, and Czechoslovakia) to America. They came to Pennsylvania, a state famous for religious freedom. The day after their arrival, they went to the statehouse in Philadelphia and swore allegiance to the King of England. And the following day they had a religious service, with a meal of thanksgiving.

The date was September 24. On that date forever since, their descendants have observed a thanksgiving holiday— called *Gedaechtnisz Tag*—to commemorate their safe arrival in America and to give thanks for the blessings of the previous year.

After the religious services, a simple meal is prepared. The menu hasn't changed for 250 years: bread, butter, and apple butter. This is traditionally considered to be the meal that was eaten at the first Schwenkfelder Thanksgiving in 1734. A recipe for Schwenkfelder Apple Butter is included at the end of this chapter.

A German cake mold.

The Pennsylvania Dutch also came from Germany. They were called that because the German word for "German" is *Deutsch*. Their Pennsylvania neighbors, mishearing the word, thought the newcomers were referring to themselves as "Dutch."

Because they disliked the Puritans of New England, the Pennsylvania Dutch scorned the "Yankee" Thanksgiving. Instead they observed an *Arnkarch*, or Harvest Home. This was a church service to bless the first fruits of the harvest, based on celebrations that they had known in Germany.

To celebrate Harvest Home, they decorated their churches with cornsilk, sheaves of wheat, the largest pumpkins and squashes from their gardens, and huge loaves of bread baked from the newly harvested grain. Church members competed to make the most gorgeous displays. At the close of the Harvest Service, special collections called "harvest thank offerings" were taken in church and later donated to charity.

The Pennsylvania Dutch believed that Thanksgiving

should come during, not after, the harvest. They observed it each year on a date (chosen by their pastors) that could fall any time between July and October. One of their objections to the "Yankee" Thanksgiving was that it came in November, too late in the year. They ignored it entirely until the twentieth century.

The people of the Virgin Islands, a United States territory in the Caribbean Sea, celebrate two thanksgivings— the national holiday and Hurricane Thanksgiving Day.

The Virgin Islands lie in the track of violent hurricanes. When the hurricane season begins, near the end of July, the islanders pray for their safety during the coming months. Then, on October 19, if there have been no hurricanes, Hurricane Thanksgiving Day is held. The islanders give thanks that they have been spared, and pray that they will be safe again during the coming year.

For many Americans, Thanksgiving is a time not only to give thanks for their blessings, but also to share those blessings with those who have been less fortunate. In the past, Thanksgiving "charity baskets" were often prepared, filled with corn, chicken, potatoes, and pumpkins. These were delivered, sometimes by children, to the homes of the needy. Today, such generosity is usually organized by churches and community groups, instead of being directly person-to-person.

And today some Americans eat *nothing* on Thanksgiving in order to remind themselves of the hunger felt by poor people around the world. Instead of spending money on a special Thanksgiving meal, they make a contribution to relieve world hunger. This, too, is a way of giving thanks.

SCHWENKFELDER APPLE BUTTER

An adaptation of a recipe used to feed the entire Schwenk-felder congregation. The original recipe required 30 pounds of sugar and 12 pails of apples. The recipe below makes 2 pints.

2 pounds apples	*¼ teaspoon cloves*
½ pound sugar	*¼ teaspoon cinnamon*
1 cup water	*⅛ teaspoon allspice*

Wash, peel, core, and quarter the apples. Cut the quarters in half.

Bring the water to a boil. Add the apples, reduce the heat to low, cover, and simmer until the apples are soft, sitrring frequently, about 1 hour. After 30 minutes, remove a few tablespoons from the pot. Stir in the spices and return the mixture to the pot. Stir well. Continue cooking until a tablespoon of sauce placed on a plate remains in place: no liquid should spread out around it. Cool and pour into containers. Store in the refrigerator. *2 pints.*

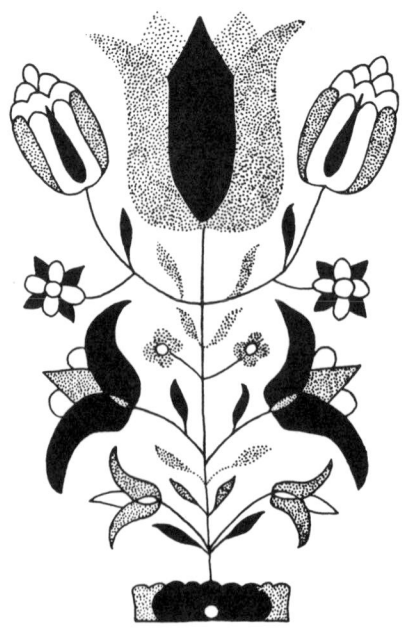

MOLASSES PIE, NEVERSINK

A favorite of the Pennsylvania Dutch.

2 nine-inch pie crusts	*3 tablespoons flour*
1 cup fine white bread crumbs	*1 teaspoon cinnamon*
⅔ cup molasses	*1 cup raisins*
½ cup honey	*6 tablespoons flour*
6 tablespoons brown sugar	*4 tablespoons brown sugar*
grated rind of ½ lemon	*2 tablespoons butter, softened*

Preheat the oven to 350°. Put 1 pie crust in a pie tin. Spread the breadcrumbs over the bottom. Spread the raisins over the crumbs.

Mix the molasses, honey, 6 tablespoons brown sugar, grated lemon rind, 3 tablespoons flour, and cinnamon. Pour this mixture over the raisins.

Mix 6 tablespoons flour, 4 tablespoons brown sugar, and 2 tablespoons softened butter. Spread over the pie.

Roll out the remaining pie crust and cut it into 1-inch strips. Make a lattice design over the pie.

Bake 40 minutes. Cool on rack. *1 pie.*

A detail from "The Harvesters" by Pieter Breugel, the Elder, 1555.

CHAPTER TEN

Thanksgiving Around the World

BECAUSE a successful harvest is supremely important— necessary, in fact, for human life to continue—some form of thanksgiving is celebrated in most countries around the world.

In northern Europe, the celebration is usually held on November 11, St. Martin's Day. St. Martin was born in Hungary in the fourth century. According to legend, he served as a soldier in France, where he was once approached by a shivering beggar. Martin tore his cloak in two and gave the beggar half of it.

That night, Jesus Christ—wearing the half-cloak that Martin had given the beggar—appeared to Martin in a vision. Martin thereupon left the army and converted to Christianity. He later became Bishop of Tours and founded a famous monastery. He is the patron saint of beggars.

In the Middle Ages, people often gave harvest feasts

for beggars on November 11, the date St. Martin was buried. And in Holland today, children sometimes pretend to be beggars on St. Martin's Day. They go from door to door, carrying lanterns and "begging" for cake, fruit, and candy. They chant:

> *Here lives a rich man*
> *Who can give us something,*
> *May he live to be very old,*
> *Have a fine death and go to paradise.*

In Sweden, St. Martin's Day is known as *Marten Gas*—Martin's Goose. The traditional feast starts with a highly spiced soup, which gets its black color and distinctive flavor from a combination of prunes and goose blood. The main course, naturally, is roast goose. For dessert there is *spettkaka*, a meringue-like cake, traditionally made by dripping strands of yellow batter onto a spit turning above a fire. Hundreds of eggs are used to make a single cake, which resembles a mound of crisp golden threads. In the evening, the children have a parade, carrying lanterns made from hollowed-out vegetables.

In Switzerland, too, children traditionally carry lanterns made from vegetables—in this case turnips. These are known as *Rabenlichter*, or "turnip lights." In the Swiss capital of Berne, a harvest festival is held on the Monday before the last Thursday in November. Farmers bring their

produce into the city to sell at booths, which they deco-
rate with flowers and with figures carved from fruits and
vegetables. Children string onions and hang them up to sell.
At the end of the festival, there is a parade through the
streets.

In Japan, harvest festivals have changed since World War II. One that has vanished entirely is *Kanname-sai*— "God-tasting Festival"—which used to be held each October 17. According to ancient legend, Kanname-sai began when Princess Yamatohime obtained some rice from a crane. She prepared a meal from it, which she offered to the Sun Goddess. In memory of that gift, rice and saki (rice wine) were offered up to the ancestors of the Royal Family each year at Kanname-sai.

Another harvest festival, *Niiname-sai*—"New-Tasting Festival"—was celebrated at the Emperor's palace each November 23. The Emperor offered the first fruits to the spirits of his ancestors. Then he tasted them and shared them with his attendants. According to legend, *Niiname-sai* originated when Prince Ninigi, known in Japanese mythology as the Imperial Grandson, came down to earth from the Celestial Abode of *Takamano-hara* and was given new rice by the local gods.

After World War II, when the Emperor ceased to be regarded as sacred, the character of this festival changed. Now it is a national holiday. Government offices are closed. People congratulate each other on the success of their farming and other occupations, and give thanks for their blessings.

"Three Ladies under Japanese Lanterns," an 18th century print by Utamaro.

Ancestor worship, a part of many religions around the world, was naturally a frequent feature of agricultural festivals.

For instance, the Ashanti people of West Africa—whose country is now called Ghana—asked permission of their ancestors even before they planted their crops. They believed that their ancestors, who had once worked the land themselves, were still its real owners.

At planting time a fowl was killed and its blood poured on the field. Then the meat of the bird was mixed with cooked yams and scattered north, south, east, and west as an offering to the Earth Mother.

Months later, after the harvest, a festival was held. It lasted for three days. But the people could not eat any of the harvest until they had offered new yams to the spirits of their ancestors. An exception was made for the children, who were allowed to eat whenever and whatever they wanted.

In India, Hindu women honored Gauri—Goddess of the Harvest and Protector of Women—with a three-day festival. On the first day, a bundle of wild balsam, an aromatic plant, was wrapped in a silk cloth. This bundle represented Gauri.

An unmarried girl carried the Gauri bundle from room to room of her family's house. The other women of the

The Emperor of India admired the turkey so much that he had this portrait painted in 1612, not long before the Pilgrims settled in the New World.

household went with her and asked repeatedly, "What have you brought?"

Depending on what room they had come to, she an-answered, "Delicious food," or "Beautiful children," or "Treasure to fill a city." The women responded, "Come on golden feet and stay forever." This ritual was thought to bring good fortune to each room visited. Afterward, the women offered milk and sweets to the Gauri bundle.

On the second day of the festival, the women feasted. On the third day, a servant took the bundle to a stream and threw it into the water. Then she gathered some earth from the banks of the stream and brought it back to the house. This earth was considered sacred, representing the soil from riverbanks where, in ancient times, the first farmers planted the first crops.

Though India is very far from England, there are many similarities between this festival and the Old English har-

A silhouette from India.

vest rites we have already seen. The bundle of wild balsam reminds us of the Kern Puppet, and throwing it into the stream is probably a rain charm. Again and again, we find similar customs practiced by people who lived thousands of miles apart, and had neither language, culture, nor climate in common. What they did share was a desire to celebrate the miracle of the harvest, and to ensure its future renewal through prayer and ceremony.

RABENLICHT
SWISS TURNIP LIGHT

1. Choose a large, ripe turnip. Cut a thin slice from the bottom so that it will sit flat.

2. Use a small, sharp knife to hollow out the center. Be careful not to cut all the way through to the bottom.

3. Working from the outside, cut out small shapes (triangles, squares, crescents, anything you like) to let the light shine through.

4. Heat the bottom of a short, thick candle until the wax is soft. Press it into the turnip and light the wick.

To make an unusual centerpiece for the Thanksgiving table, put the turnip light on a flat dish and surround it with other vegetables and fruits.

WEST AFRICAN YAM SOUP

Yams are a major food source in West Africa. They are cooked in many different ways—boiled, mashed, fried, dried, ground into flour, and used to flavor soups and stews. This yam soup has an unusual, sweet flavor and a pretty orange-yellow color.

2 tablespoons butter
½ cup onion, chopped
4 cups chicken broth

3 cups yams peeled and diced
salt and pepper
pinch of cayenne

Melt the butter in a heavy saucepan. Add the onion and cook until golden. Set aside.

Bring the broth to a boil. Add the yams. Cover, reduce heat, and simmer until the yams are tender, about 20 minutes. Drain the yams. Reserve the liquid.

Put the yams through a sieve or purée them in the blender. Mix the yams, cooking liquid, onion, salt, pepper, and cayenne. Serve hot. *Serves 8.*

Carved wooden containers from Africa and the knife used to make them.

CHAPTER ELEVEN

The Thanksgiving Feast

Here is an assortment of Thanksgiving recipes. Many are adaptations of early colonial favorites. Others are more recent regional specialties.

All are delicious, and I hope that you will enjoy preparing and eating them.

Turkey

Wild turkeys once ranged over most of North and South America. They have existed for about ten million years— far longer than human beings.

Turkeys were domesticated by the Aztecs, who called them *uexolotl* and kept them for food. Spanish explorers and soldiers brought them home from Mexico to Europe.

Where did the name "turkey" come from? Many explanations have been suggested.

—The bird is named after the country of Turkey.

—Columbus, when he first arrived in the New World, thought he had come to India. He assumed that the wild turkeys must be peacocks. So he called them *tuka*, which is the word for peacock in Tamil, a language of India.

—Luis de Torres, a doctor who served with Columbus on his first voyage to America, named the bird *tukki*, which means "big bird" in Hebrew.

—"Firkee," the bird's name in one of the languages of the North American Indians, was corrupted to "turkey."

—The name comes from the bird's call when it is frightened: *turc turc turc turc turc*.

However the turkey got its name, early settlers had good reason to be interested in wild turkeys. Because of their size—twenty to thirty pounds—and because they were easy to kill or catch, wild turkeys became an important source of food. They can fly fast, but usually don't fly far. Instead they try to hide in tall grass, where hunters can easily find them—so easily that wild turkeys have come close to extinction. But as a result of recent laws that restrict their hunting, they are now increasing in number.

The settlers found that turkeys could be trapped as well as shot. Their method was simple. They would build a covered pen, and cut a turkey-sized hole in one wall. Then they would lure the turkeys with a trail of corn. The turkeys would eat their way along the trail, through the hole, and into the pen. At this point they would look up, but, having poor eyesight, could not see the way out.

Wild turkeys remained plentiful and extremely cheap for two hundred years—so much so that some people despised them as "common" food. In fact, until the twentieth century, the supply of turkey meat so greatly exceeded the demand for it that the object of turkey breeding was not to develop a meaty bird, but rather to perfect the wild turkey's beautiful feathers, used to adorn hats and gowns. Today, breeders emphasize the quality and amount of meat. Large-breasted turkeys with plenty of white meat are considered most desirable.

A fashionable feathered hat from the 18th century.

The turkey was almost chosen over the eagle as the symbol of America.

Americans eat 535 million pounds of turkey every Thanksgiving. Turkey meat is appreciated not only because of its delicious taste, but also because it is highly nutritious and low in calories. Protein-rich, it has high concentrations of the B vitamins, niacin, and riboflavin, as well as valuable amounts of calcium, iron, vitamin A, and vitamin C.

After the United States won its independence, Congress debated the choice of a national bird, and Benjamin Franklin advocated the turkey instead of the bald eagle. He called the eagle a bird of bad moral character. The turkey, on the other hand, he considered "a much more respectable bird and withal a true native of America."

ROAST TURKEY

Here are general directions for thawing frozen turkeys, for stuffing turkeys, and for roasting them. Recipes for stuffings follow.

1. Freezing preserves food and prevents the growth of bacteria. So when you bring home a frozen turkey, be sure to *keep* it frozen until the time has come to start preparing it.

2. A frozen turkey may be thawed in the refrigerator. It takes about two days for a turkey of twelve pounds or more to defrost.

An illustration by Paul Revere, from a cookbook published in 1772.

Or you can place the turkey *in its original wrapping* inside a large paper bag. Put this package in a shallow tray and leave it on a kitchen counter. The bag should be closed, keeping the outside of the bird cool (to retard the growth of bacteria) while the center is thawing. Allow twenty-four hours for a large turkey.

A faster way is to place the turkey *in its original wrapping* under cool running water. A large turkey will thaw in seven or eight hours.

3. Remove whatever giblets (organs) you find within the body cavity; these will probably be wrapped in paper. Rinse the turkey thoroughly, inside and out, with cool running water. Pat it dry with paper towels.

4. If you are stuffing the turkey, spoon stuffing into the body cavity and sew it up or fasten it with skewers. Be careful not to pack the stuffing tightly: it expands as it cooks. Tie the drumsticks together.

5. Place the turkey on a rack in a shallow roasting pan, breast side up. Moisten the skin by spooning on melted butter, or brush it on with a pastry brush.

6. Roast the turkey at 325°. Because the oven temperature will drop sharply when you first put the turkey in, it's a good idea—especially with a large turkey—to preheat the oven to 450°, lowering the temperature to 325° when you put in the turkey.

7. To help you judge when the turkey is done, a meat thermometer is helpful, though not absolutely necessary. Insert its point into the center of the stuffing. If you don't stuff the turkey, insert the thermometer into the inside thigh muscle, making sure it doesn't touch the bone. When it reaches 190°, the turkey is done.

8. If you don't use a thermometer, you can tell when the turkey is done by piercing the thigh with a fork. The juices should *not* be red. They should run clear. Another test is to jiggle the drumsticks up and down; they should move easily when the turkey is fully cooked.

   A small turkey, eight pounds or under, will need to cook twenty minutes per pound. A larger bird should be cooked for fifteen minutes per pound. If the turkey is stuffed, add five minutes per pound.

9. Baste the turkey often with the drippings in the pan. If the breast gets brown so quickly that you're afraid it will burn, cover it with a "tent" of aluminum foil. When you think the turkey will soon be ready to come out, you can remove the tent in order to get any additional browning that you desire.

10. When the turkey is done, remove it from the pan to a warm platter.

11. To make gravy, strain the pan juices and skim off the fat. (Skimming the fat will become easier as the liquid cools.) Heat four tablespoons of the fat and stir in four

tablespoons of flour. Heat and stir until the mixture is smooth. Add two cups of pan juices. Stir until the gravy is smooth, then simmer until it thickens, about five minutes.

12. Remove the skewers or stitches from the turkey. Spoon the stuffing into a bowl and carve the turkey. Refrigerate any leftovers promptly, because turkey that has been stuffed goes bad quickly.

If you have leftovers—don't worry! The recipe for Pennsylvania Dutch Turkey Scallop is a good way of using leftover turkey. After you try it, you may decide that it's *always* a good idea to cook a large turkey.

PILGRIM STUFFING

The English colonists liked a rich, sweet, pudding-like mixture tinted with food dyes: spinach juice for green, saffron for yellow, berry juice for red or purple. This stuffing might well have been prepared by an early Colonial housewife.

1 cup heavy cream	*¼ teaspoon mace*
2 egg yolks	*¼ teaspoon nutmeg*
1 tablespoon honey	*½ teaspoon salt*
pinch of saffron (optional)	*1¼ cups fine bread crumbs*
½ teaspoon cinnamon	*1 cup currants or raisins*

Beat the cream, egg yolks, honey, and saffron vigorously with a fork. Stir in the spices and salt. Add the bread crumbs. Mix well. Stir in the currants or raisins. Stuff the turkey according to the directions on page 116.   *3 cups.*

Cinnamon was a popular ingredient in 17th century recipes. This old print shows the spice being harvested in Borneo.

PECAN STUFFING

2 tablespoons butter
turkey giblets
6 cups whole wheat bread
  crumbs
1½ teaspoons salt
1 teaspoon black pepper
1 teaspoon cloves

¼ teaspoon cayenne
½ cup butter, melted
2 cups boiling water
2 tablespoons honey
4 eggs, beaten
3 cups pecans, chopped

Melt 2 tablespoons butter in a heavy skillet over medium heat. Add the giblets and brown on all sides. Cool. Dice the cooked giblets and set aside.

Mix the bread crumbs, salt, pepper, and spices. Stir in the melted butter, boiling water, and honey. Cool. Add the beaten eggs. Mix well. Stir in the cooked giblets and chopped pecans.

Stuff the turkey according to the directions on page 116.

8 cups.

CORNBREAD STUFFING

2 cups cornbread crumbs
2 cups white bread crumbs
2 cups chicken broth
3 eggs
½ cup milk

½ cup butter, melted and
  cooled
1 cup celery, chopped
1 cup onion, chopped
salt and pepper

Mix cornbread crumbs and white bread crumbs in a large bowl. Stir in the chicken broth.

Beat the eggs and add to the crumb mixture. Add the milk and melted butter. Stir in the celery and onions. Season to taste with salt and pepper.

Stuff the turkey according to the directions on page 116.

6 cups.

DUTCH TURKEY SCALLOP

This is a marvelous way to use up Thanksgiving leftovers!

2 cups cooked turkey, diced
2 cups leftover stuffing
4 hardboiled eggs, peeled and sliced

butter
1 cup gravy
2 tablespoons milk

Preheat oven to 350°. Butter a 1½-quart casserole.

Spread a layer of stuffing in the bottom of the casserole. Add a layer of diced turkey, then a layer of sliced eggs. Dot with butter. Continue to add layers of stuffing, turkey, eggs, and butter dots. Finish with a layer of stuffing.

Mix the gravy and milk. Pour over the top of the casserole. Dot with butter. Cover and bake 30 minutes. Remove the cover and broil 2 to 3 minutes, until the top of the scallop is browned. *Serves 4.*

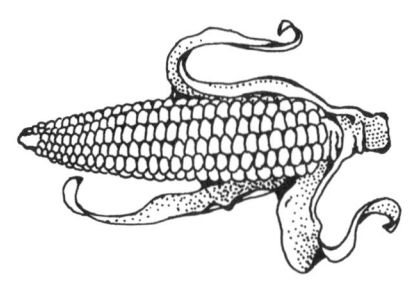

Corn

In 1492, when Columbus landed in Cuba, some of his sailors went ashore to explore. They came back with the news that the natives were cultivating a strange and wonderful plant.

In the native language it was called *mahiz*. The closest the Spaniards could come was *maiz*. The English version of the Spanish word was "maize." The English also called it "Indian corn." Americans today simply call it "corn."

Columbus brought corn plants back to Europe. At first corn seemed very foreign to the farmers of the Old World, and the names they gave it express various theories about its origin. In France, it was called "Spanish corn"; in Egypt, "Syrian corn"; in Turkey, "Egyptian wheat"; and in Holland, "Turkish wheat."

Soon corn was being grown in parts of Europe (though the Pilgrims seem never to have seen it before their arrival in America), from where its cultivation spread to Africa, India, and China. By the sixteenth century, corn was so well-established in China that the emperor was already taxing it.

There are three principal types of corn: feed corn (used mostly to feed animals), sweet corn (the corn we eat), and popcorn.

Do you think of popcorn as a modern invention? In a bat cave in Mexico, archeologists found popped corn that was 5,600 years old. Some thousand-year-old unpopped kernels were found in Peru—and could still be popped.

The Indians had several different ways of popping corn. Sometimes they skewered an ear and held it over the fire. Or they sliced the kernels off the cob and threw them directly into the flames. As the kernels popped they jumped out in all directions, and the children chased and gathered them.

These methods were quick, but many kernels were simply burned up and lost. A better way was to fill a clay

A corn jar from Peru.

pot with hot sand, add the popcorn kernels, and stir. As the kernels popped they shot to the top of the pot and were removed.

The Indians loved popcorn. They ate it plain, as we do, or used it to garnish soups and stews. Columbus found Indians in El Salvador *wearing* popcorn as jewelry.

Because it changes form so suddenly and dramatically, like hardly anything else in the natural world, popcorn has given rise to many myths and stories. One Indian belief was that a little demon lived in each kernel. When his house was heated, he blew up!

Corn-husking was not only a necessary chore for the colonists, it was also a social event.

MASHED SWEET POTATOES

Mashed sweet potatoes are the basis for several of the recipes that follow. They are easy to prepare and good to eat with butter and salt or a spoonful of honey.

6 medium-sized sweet potatoes

Wash the potatoes and cut them into quarters. Cut the quarters in half. Place in a heavy saucepan, cover with very hot water, and boil gently until potatoes are tender, 20–30 minutes. Drain well. Remove and discard the peels. Mash with a potato masher or fork until potatoes are smooth and fluffy. Season to taste with butter, salt, and honey.   *2–3 cups.*

STUFFED SWEET POTATOES

Sweet potatoes, apples, and maple syrup are blended elegantly in this harvest vegetable dish.

4 medium-sized sweet potatoes   *¼ cup coconut*
2 apples   *2 tablespoons maple syrup*
1 tablespoon fresh lemon juice   *4 tablespoons butter, melted*

Preheat the oven to 400°.

Wash and dry the potatoes. Rub their skins with butter and bake 1 hour. Cut each potato in half lengthwise and scoop out the pulp. Be careful not to tear the skins. Mash the pulp with a fork.

Wash, peel, core, and grate the apples. Sprinkle them with the lemon juice. Mix the apples, coconut, maple syrup, and melted butter into the mashed potatoes. Replace the mixture in the skins. Return to the oven and broil briefly until the tops are lightly browned.   *Serves 8.*

PENNSYLVANIA DUTCH
GREEN CORN SOUP

This soup should be made only with fresh corn. The young, "green" corn, harvested at the beginning of the season, is best, but any fresh corn may be used.

3 tablespoons butter	*2 egg yolks*
1½ cups fresh corn kernels	*large pretzels*
12 cups chicken broth	

Melt the butter in a heavy pot. Add the corn kernels and stir over low heat to coat them with butter. Add the chicken broth. Bring to a boil. Reduce the heat, cover, and simmer for two hours. Strain the soup through a fine sieve. Stir in the egg yolks. Pour the soup into bowls and garnish each one with a large pretzel. *Serves 8 to 10.*

CORN DODGERS

1 cup cornmeal	*2 tablespoons melted butter*
1 teaspoon salt	*1 cup boiling water*
1½ teaspoons sugar	

Preheat oven to 400°. Butter a cookie sheet.

Mix cornmeal, salt, and sugar. Stir in melted butter and boiling water. Continue to stir until the mixture is smooth.

Wet your hands in cold water. Shape handfuls of the cornmeal mixture to resemble short, fat sausages. Wet your hands frequently to prevent the batter from sticking. Place the dodgers on the buttered cookie sheet and bake until golden, about 15 minutes. *Makes 15 to 20 dodgers.*

POPCORN CAKE MENNONITE

2 quarts popped corn
2½ cups nuts, chopped
½ cup butter

¼ cup water
2½ cups powdered sugar

Butter an 8-inch round cake pan. Mix the popped corn and nuts. Set aside. Bring ¼ cup water to a boil.

Melt the butter in a heavy saucepan. Add the ¼ cup water. Stir in the sugar. Cook, stirring constantly, over medium heat until the mixture reaches 270° on a candy thermometer. Carefully pour the hot syrup over the popcorn mixture. Stir *immediately*, gently but thoroughly. Spoon a layer of the mixture into the buttered cake pan. Press it down with a spatula. Add another layer and press again. Continue until the pan is full. Cool and slice. *Serves 8 to 10.*

Sweet Potatoes

Sweet potatoes, a native American vegetable, startled the early settlers. One eighteenth-century writer described them as "about as long as a Boy's Leg, and sometimes as long and big as both the Leg and Thigh of a Young Child and very much resembling it in Shape."

In fact, sweet potatoes really aren't potatoes at all. They are the enlarged, fleshy roots of a vine called *Ipomoea Batatas*, a member of the morning-glory family with beautiful pink or violet flowers.

Sweet potatoes vary widely in color. The insides range from almost white to orange, the outsides from light brown to purplish red. South American Indians mixed the reddest sweet potatoes with lime juice to make a handsome dye.

In colonial days, sweet potatoes were an important crop and housewives devised various ways of cooking them. At first they were simply roasted in the ashes on the hearth. By the nineteenth century, candied sweet potatoes had become a popular dish. The cooked meat was scooped out of the skin, mixed with lemon juice or orange juice (or chopped apple or coconut), and reheated. In New England, the meat was sometimes mashed with maple syrup.

Sweet potatoes are rich in starch. The orange varieties also contain large amounts of carotene, a substance that turns to vitamin A in the body.

The warm autumnal color of sweet potatoes makes them an especially attractive addition to the Thanksgiving table.

"Marion feasting the British officer on sweet potatoes," an oil painting by G.W. Mark, 1848.

SWEET POTATO PIE

The top of this candy-like pie will puff up like a soufflé as it bakes and then flatten as it cools.

1 nine-inch pie crust
1 egg white
1 cup sweet potatoes, cooked and mashed
1 cup heavy cream
½ cup light corn syrup
½ teaspoon salt

½ cup brown sugar, packed
2 tablespoons honey
3 eggs, lightly beaten
finely grated rind of 1 small orange
2 tablespoons orange juice

Preheat the oven to 425°.

Brush the pie crust with egg white. Set aside.

Mix the sweet potatoes and heavy cream. Add the corn syrup, salt, brown sugar, and honey. Beat until the mixture is smooth. Stir in the eggs, grated orange rind, and orange juice. Pour the batter into the pie crust.

Bake 10 minutes. Reduce the heat to 350° and bake until a knife inserted into the center comes out clean, 20–30 minutes.

1 pie.

SWEET POTATO CUSTARD

An unusual vegetable side dish to serve with turkey.

*2 cups sweet potatoes, cooked
and mashed*
2 tablespoons honey
1 tablespoon butter, softened

2 eggs, lightly beaten
1 cup milk
½ teaspoon lemon extract

Preheat the oven to 350°.

Mix the potatoes, honey, butter, eggs, and milk. Stir in the lemon extract.

Butter a 9-inch pie plate. Pour in the batter. Bake until a knife inserted into the center comes out clean, about 1 hour. Serve warm or cold.

Serves 8.

A baker in the early 1800's.

Pumpkin

A Fairy Seed I planted
  So dry and white and old;
There sprang a vine enchanted
  With magic flowers of gold.

I watched it, I tended it,
  And truly by and by
It bore a Jack O'Lantern
  And a great Thanksgiving pie.

—"The Magic Vine"
Anonymous

The Indians had many uses for pumpkins. In addition to cooking and eating the flesh, they dried the seeds, which are especially nutritious. These they ate as a cereal, or ground up and baked into cakes. Sometimes the hollowed-out shells were carved into masks, much the same way we make Jack O'Lanterns.

Pumpkins have the special virtue of growing well in small gardens together with corn and beans. An Indian legend tells of the Corn Lady and her two would-be husbands—the Bean and the Pumpkin. When she finally agreed to marry the Bean, he put his arms around her. The Pumpkin sank down to hide his sorrow. And that, according to the legend, is why beans climb cornstalks, while pumpkin vines wander along the earth between the rows.

The colonists were delighted to learn about pumpkins, which grow well under practically any conditions. They ate so many pumpkins, in fact, that one of them composed this ditty:

> *We have pumpkin at morning*
> *And pumpkin at noon,*
> *If it was not for pumpkin*
> *We would be undoon.*

BAKED PUMPKIN

Here is how to prepare cooked pumpkin, which is called for in some of the following recipes.

1. Wash a medium pumpkin and cut it in half. Remove the seeds (you may save them to make Roasted Pumpkin Seeds, below) and the soft pulp clinging to them.

2. Place the halves in a buttered baking dish, skin side up. Bake until tender (about 1 hour). The pumpkin is cooked when you can easily cut its meat with a fork.

3. Scrape the meat from the skin. Press it through a sieve with the back of a spoon to remove the fibers.

ROASTED PUMPKIN SEEDS

1 medium pumpkin   *1½ tablespoons butter*

Preheat the oven to 250°.

Remove the seeds from the pumpkin. You may save the pulp for another pumpkin recipe.

Clean off the soft fibers that cling to the seeds. For each 2 cups of seeds, melt 1½ tablespoons of butter in a shallow pan. Add seeds and stir until they are lightly coated with butter.

Bake, stirring occasionally, until the seeds are crisp and brown, about 15 minutes. Cool and store in an air-tight container.

PRESERVED PUMPKIN CHIPS

This unusual sweet is an adaptation of a recipe from Miss Eliza Leslie's *Seventy-Five Receipts For Pastry, Cake, and Sweet-meats*, published in 1833.

1 medium pumpkin	*1 cup fresh lemon juice*
2 cups sugar	*grated rind of 2 large lemons*

Cut the pumpkin into quarters. Remove the seeds and any soft fibers that cling to them. Peel off the skin and discard. Cut the flesh into thin chips about 1½ inches square. Measure 4 cups of chips. Put them in a shallow bowl.

Stir the lemon juice into the sugar and pour the mixture over the chips. Cover and let stand overnight.

In the morning, transfer the chips and lemon juice to a heavy 2-quart saucepan. Bring to a boil. Skim off the foam with a wooden spoon. Reduce the heat, cover, and boil gently until the chips are tender, about 1 hour. Transfer the chips to a plate, using a slotted spoon. Continue to boil the syrup until it thickens, about 15 minutes. Skim off the foam. Put the chips back in the pan and boil 10 minutes longer. Remove from the heat. Cool. Stir in the lemon rind.

Put the chips and syrup in a covered glass jar. Store in the refrigerator.

Serve over lemon sherbet. Or use to garnish slices of pumpkin pie or bowls of pumpkin soup. *1 pint.*

PUMPKIN FRITTERS

1 tablespoon butter
1 tablespoon corn oil
1 cup cooked or canned
  pumpkin
¼ teaspoon salt
⅛ teaspoon black pepper

pinch of cayenne
1 egg, lightly beaten
½ cup flour
¼ cup milk
½ small green pepper, seeded
  and chopped

Heat butter and corn oil in a heavy frying pan.

Mix remaining ingredients together. Drop tablespoonfuls of the batter into the hot pan. The fritters should not touch each other. Cook over medium heat until the bottoms are lightly browned. Turn the fritters and cook the other side. Serve at once. *20 fritters.*

PUMPKIN PIE

*What moistens the lip
And brightens the eye;
What calls back the past
Like rich pumpkin pie?*

—"The Pumpkin,"

JOHN GREENLEAF WHITTIER

1 9-inch pie crust, unbaked
1 egg white
2 eggs
½ cup brown sugar, packed
1 tablespoon molasses
½ teaspoon salt

1 teaspoon cinnamon
½ teaspoon cloves
½ teaspoon ginger
2 cups cooked or canned
  pumpkin
1½ cups milk

Preheat the oven to 450°.

Brush the pie crust with egg white. Set aside.

Beat the eggs. Stir in the brown sugar, molasses, salt, and spices. Add the pumpkin and milk. Mix well. Pour into the pie crust. It will be very full.

Bake 15 minutes. Reduce the heat to 350° and bake until a knife inserted into the center comes out clean, about 1 hour. Cool. You can garnish slices of the pie with preserved pumpkin chips, page 137.   *1 pie.*

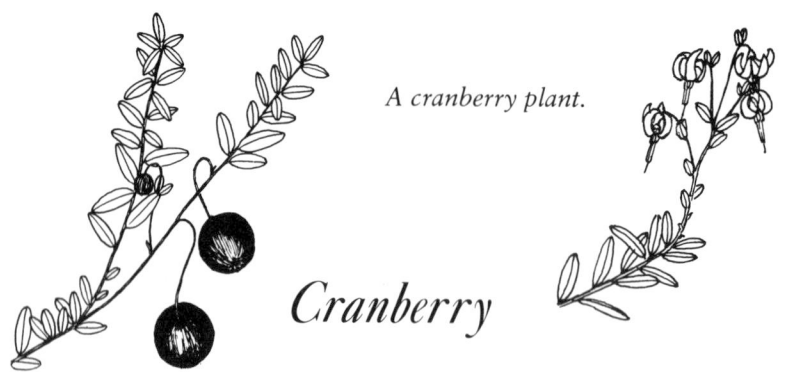

A cranberry plant.

Cranberry

Our English word "cranberry" comes from the German *kraanbere*, meaning "crane-berry." But it is not clear why German settlers chose that name for this small, sour, crimson berry.

It may be that they thought the cranberry blossom resembled the head and beak of a crane. Or perhaps it was because cranberries were the favorite food of cranes.

In colonial times, wild cranberries grew abundantly in swampy areas near the coast as far south as Virginia. The Indians used them for food, medicine, and dye. Sometimes they preserved them by pounding and shaping them into cakes that they dried in the sun. When they needed them later, to use in soups and stews and batters, they simply added a little water to soften the dried cakes.

Europeans found the plain berries too bitter to eat by themselves, but discovered that they liked them mixed with maple syrup. And when regular supplies of white and brown sugar began arriving from plantations in the West Indies, cranberries became a staple of the colonial diet.

Were cranberries part of the first Thanksgiving meal in 1621? We can't be certain, but the berries would have been ripe at that season. And we do know that cranberries appeared at later Thanksgiving feasts throughout the New England colonies.

Every cranberry eaten in colonial times and for many years afterward had to be picked wild. Farmers found them impossible to grow.

For one thing, it was too expensive to create the bogs that cranberries need. This problem was finally solved by mounding peat on top of large pumps, which flood and drain the vines as required.

Another problem was that cranberries are difficult to harvest. They must be picked by hand or with a scope, a large rake-like tool. And damaged berries must be separated from the good ones. For years, this was done slowly and carefully by hand.

A grower called Peg-Leg is supposed to have found an easier way. His wooden leg made it hard to carry baskets of berries down flights of steps, so he simply poured them down. He noticed that the firm berries bounced to the bottom, while the soft, bruised ones were left behind. Peg-Leg's observation explains the principle of the mechanical cranberry sorter. Even today, cranberry grading machines depend on the fact that good cranberries bounce.

Today, as many as three hundred bushels of cranberries can be harvested from a single acre. More than half of the crop is made into sauce, which is canned. The rest is sold fresh or made into pies, relish, or juice.

Cranberries and cranberry juice are excellent sources

A crane.

of vitamin C. Early sea captains carried barrels of dried berries on long voyages to protect their crews against scurvy. After months at sea—or even years, in the case of whaling expeditions—cranberries still retained their nutritional value.

When cooking with fresh cranberries, sort them carefully. Remove any that are bruised or shriveled. Wash the good ones in cold water and drain them well before you use them.

FRESH CRANBERRY JUICE

1½ pounds cranberries   *⅔ cup sugar*

Put washed cranberries in a heavy saucepan. Add enough water to cover them. Bring to a boil. Reduce the heat, cover, and boil gently until the berries are soft, about 10 minutes. Stir and mash them occasionally with a fork.

Strain the cooked mixture. You will have about 2 cups of juice. Stir in the sugar. Replace the juice in the saucepan and bring to a boil. Reduce the heat, cover, and boil gently 15 minutes longer. Cool and store in the refrigerator. The juice will be strong. Add water to taste before serving.   *1½ pints.*

CRANBERRY SAUCE

Here's a colonial recipe for a traditional Thanksgiving favorite.

12 ounces (about 3 cups)
  cranberries
1½ cups boiling water

1½ cups brown sugar
1 tablespoon freshly grated
  lemon peel

Put the cranberries in a heavy 2½ quart saucepan. Cover with the boiling water. Bring to a second boil over medium-high heat. Cover, reduce the heat, and simmer until the skins burst, about 3 minutes. Gently stir in the sugar. Remove from heat. Cool. Stir in lemon peel. Chill in refrigerator overnight before serving. *2 pints.*

CRANBERRY CONSERVE

A tasty recipe from Fanny Pierson Crane's eighteenth-century cookbook.

4 cups fresh cranberries
1 large orange
1 cup golden raisins
¼ cup honey

¾ cup sugar
1½ teaspoons ginger
½ cup walnuts, chopped

Wash the orange and cut it into quarters. Remove the seeds. Put the orange and washed cranberries through a food chopper or chop by hand. Mix the chopped fruit, raisins, honey, sugar, ginger, and walnuts. Chill in the refrigerator for at least 4 hours before serving so that the flavors will blend together. *4 cups.*

CRANBERRY ICE CREAM

1 small lemon   *1 cup heavy cream*
1 cup sugar   *pinch of salt*
                                         1 cup cranberry juice*

Grate the lemon and squeeze out the juice. Set grated rind and juice aside.

Stir the sugar into the cream. Add the salt. Stir in the cranberry juice and lemon juice. Stir in the grated rind.

Pour the mixture into a 9-inch pie plate and place in the freezer. When the mixture is frozen around the edges but still soft in the center, spoon it into a cold bowl. Beat it with cold beaters. (You can chill the bowl and beaters in the freezer.) Replace the cranberry mixture in the pie pan and freeze again until partly frozen. Return to the cold bowl and again beat with cold beaters. Replace in the freezer and freeze completely.

1½ pints.

*If you follow the recipe for making cranberry juice on page 142, don't add the sugar or boil a second time. If you wish, you may use canned cranberry juice instead.

Apples

Europeans cultivated apple orchards for hundreds of years before the discovery of America. So it was natural that early colonists brought apple seeds and young trees with them. Orchards were quickly planted and grew so well that apples became a staple American food.

Wherever settlers moved as they spread across the continent, they planted apple trees. One man, Jonathan Chapman of Boston, collected apple seeds from cider mills, dried them, and gave them to people going west. Eventually he too traveled across the country, sowing apple seeds wherever he went. Today we remember him as Johnny Appleseed.

Now every state in the union—and every country in the world with a temperate climate—grows apples. There are thousands of varieties: some for cider and juice, some for pies and sauces, some simply for eating fresh off the stem. These last are called dessert apples.

When buying apples, choose firm, unblemished ones. Refrigerate them in plastic bags that have holes poked in them. If you have too many to fit in the refrigerator, wrap them individually in tissue paper and store them in a cool, dark place. If you put them in boxes, the sides of the boxes should be made of mesh or slats of wood separated by gaps. Good air circulation is important.

The best varieties of apples for baking and for making into applesauce include Golden Delicious, Rome Beauty, Cortland, Stayman, York Imperial, and Jonathan apples. Among the most popular dessert apples are Golden Delicious, Red Delicious, Northern Spy, Winesap, and McIntosh.

Apples blend well with a remarkable variety of foods. They are high in pectin, malic acid, minerals, and vitamin C. And dentists praise apples—besides not causing cavities, apples actually help keep teeth clean with their abrasive polishing action.

BAKED APPLES FOR GARNISH

6 small red apples

Preheat the oven to 350°.

Wash the apples. Place them, stems up, in a baking pan. Add 2 inches of hot water and bake 20 minutes. The apples will still be quite firm.   *6 baked apples.*

APPLE PANDOWDY

1 cup flour
2 teaspoons baking powder
½ teaspoon salt
½ teaspoon cinnamon

1 cup brown sugar, packed
1 cup milk
4 cups apples, thinly sliced

Preheat the oven to 350°.

Sift together the flour, baking powder, salt, and cinnamon. Work in the brown sugar with your fingers. Add the milk. Stir until smooth. Set aside.

Butter a 9-inch square baking pan. Arrange the sliced apples in the bottom. Pour the batter evenly over the top. Bake until the top springs back when lightly pressed with a fingertip, 50–60 minutes. Serve hot or cold. *Serves 8.*

APPLE PORCUPINE

In an emergency, porcupines are edible. Because they are slow-moving animals, easy to catch, their meat—which is said to taste like pork—can save the lives of travelers lost in the snow. In order to preserve them for this purpose, porcupines were legally protected from hunters in Vermont. But this sweet "porcupine," made of apples and meringue, was available to all.

9 medium apples, baked*
½ cup currant jelly
1 tablespoon water
2 egg whites

¼ teaspoon cream of tartar
3 tablespoons sugar
pinch of salt
½ cup sliced almonds

Preheat the oven to 350°. Butter an 8-inch round baking dish. Cut the apples in half. Remove the seeds and cores.

Stir the jelly and water in a small sauce pan over low heat until the mixture is smooth.

In the buttered baking dish, pile the apple halves (skin side up) in the shape of a porcupine. As you position each apple, paint the top with the warm jelly mixture. Set aside.

Beat the egg whites, cream of tartar, sugar, and salt until stiff. Gently coat the apple mound with the mixture. Stick in the almonds close together to resemble a porcupine's quills. Bake in the oven until lightly browned, about 30 minutes.

Serves 6 to 8.

*You may follow the instructions for baked apples on page 146, but increase the baking time until the apples can be easily pierced with a fork.

Picture Acknowledgments

By permission of the American Museum of Natural History, 45, 48.

Courtesy of the Abby Aldrich Rockefeller Folk Art Collection, Williamsburg, Virginia, 135.

Courtesy of the Biblioteca Laureziana, Florence, 40.

By permission of the Bodleian Library, from the Codex Mendoza manuscript, Ms. Arch. Seld. A.1, folio 16 recto detail, 10.

By permission of the Trustees of the British Museum, 13, 28–29, 38, 64, 79, 121.

Courtesy of Grandma Moses Properties Co., (Grandma Moses, *Thanksgiving Turkey*, 1943. Copyright © 1982, Grandma Moses Properties Co., New York) and the Metropolitan Museum of Art, Bequest of Mary Stillman Harkness, 1950. (50. 145. 375), 12.

From the collection of Walter J. Donnelly, 60, 65, 73.

Courtesy of the Folger Library, 74.

Courtesy of the Free Library of Philadelphia, Rosenbach Collection, 84.

By permission of the Guildhall Library, City of London, 83.

Courtesy of the John Hancock Mutual Life Insurance Company, 80–81.

By permission of the Library of Congress, 22, 54, 68, 77, 114.

Courtesy of the Metropolitan Museum of Art, Rogers Fund, 1919 (19.164), 102; H.O. Havemeyer, Bequest of Mrs. H.O. Havemeyer, 1920 (JP 1658), 107.

Courtesy of the Museum of the American Indian, Heye Foundation, 43, 49, 57, 125.

Courtesy of the National Gallery of Art, Gift of Edgar William and Bernice Chrysler Garbisch, 14, 131; Index of American Design, 98.

Courtesy of the New York Historical Society, 2 ("Portrait of Miss Frances Taylor with Unidentified Man and Glass of Wine," 1831), 8, 56, 70.

The New York Public Library Picture Collection, 14, 21, 22, 24–25, 26, 30–31, 31 (bottom), 34–35, 41, 44, 67, 71, 82, 101, 105, 111, 112, 115, 126, 141.

Courtesy of the Peabody Museum of Salem, Massachusetts, 17 (top), 95.

Courtesy of the Philbrook Art Center, Tulsa, Oklahoma, 46.

Courtesy of the A.H. Robins Co., painting by John Hull, 87.

Courtesy of the Smithsonian Institution National Anthropological Archives, 50, 51, 52.

Courtesy of the Victoria and Albert Museum, London, 109.

By permission of the Yale University Library, engraving by Alexander Anderson, 91.

Selected Bibliography

Aresty, Esther B. *The Delectable Past*. New York: Simon & Schuster, 1964.

Booth, Sally. *Hung, Strung, and Potted*. New York: Clarkson N. Potter, Publisher, 1971.

Carter, W. H. *North American Indian Games*. London, Ontario, Canada: Namind Printers and Publishers, 1974.

Deetz, James, and Jay Anderson. "Partakers of Plenty: A Study of the First Thanksgiving." *Plimoth Plantation Educational Publication Series*.

Driver, Harold E. *Indians of North America*. Chicago and London: University of Chicago Press, 1969.

Earle, Alice Morse. *Home Life in Colonial Days*. Middle Village, New York: Jonathan David Publishers, Inc., 1975.

Edwards, Everett E. and Wayne D. Rasmussen. "Bibliography of the Agriculture of the American Indians." *United States Department of Agriculture Miscellaneous Publication #447*, 1942.

Frazer, James. *The Golden Bough*. New York: The Macmillan Company, 1922.

James, E. O. *Seasonal Feasts and Festivals*. New York: Barnes and Noble, Inc., 1961.

Kavasch, Barrie. *Native Harvests*. New York: Random House, 1977.

Kimball, Marie. *Thomas Jefferson's Cookbook*. Richmond, Virginia: Garrett and Massie, Publishers, 1949.

Kimball, Yeffe and Jean Anderson. *The Art of American Indian Cooking*. Garden City, New York: Doubleday, 1964.

Love, W. DeLoss Jr. *The Fast and Thanksgiving Days of New England*. Cambridge: Houghton Mifflin and Company. The Riverside Press, 1895.

Lowenberg, Miriam E. et al. *Food and Man*. New York: John Wiley and Sons, 1974.

Miller, John C. *The Colonial Image*. New York: George Braziller, 1962.

Myers, Robert. *Celebrations: The Complete Book of American Holidays*. New York: Doubleday, 1972.

Niethammer, Carolyn. *American Indian Food and Lore*. New York: Collier Books, 1974.

Nylander, Jane C. "Thanksgiving in New England—a Cornucopia of Memories, Traditions, and Food." *Rural Visitor*, Fall, 1981.

Root, Waverly, and Richard de Rochemont. *Eating in America*. New York: William Morrow and Company, Inc., 1976.

Schauffler, Robert Haven, ed. *Thanksgiving*. New York: Dodd, Mead and Company, 1943.

Simmons, Amelia. *American Cookery*. Facsimile of the original 1796 edition. Grand Rapids, Michigan: William B. Erdmans Publishing Company, Inc., 1965.

Thomas, Gertrude I. *Foods of our Forefathers*. Philadelphia: F. A. Davis Company, Publishers, 1941.

Van Doren, Mark, ed. *Travels of William Bartram*. New York: Dover Publications, Inc., 1928.

Verrill, A. Hyatt. *Foods America Gave the World*. Boston: L. C. Page and Company, 1937.

Whistler, Lawrence. *The English Festivals*. London: William Heinemann, Ltd., 1947.

Willison, George F. *Saints and Strangers*. New York: Reynal and Hitchcock, 1945.

Witthoft, John. *Green Corn Ceremonialism in the Eastern Woodlands*. Ann Arbor: University of Michigan Press, 1949.

Index